THE TWO CONSTITUTIONS

THE TWO CONSTITUTIONS

A COMPARATIVE STUDY OF BRITISH AND AMERICAN CONSTITUTIONAL SYSTEMS

by

HAROLD STANNARD

M.A., Oxon.

ADAM AND CHARLES BLACK
4, 5 & 6 SOHO SQUARE LONDON W.1

THIS EDITION FIRST PUBLISHED 1949, A. & C. BLACK, LTD.
REPRINTED 1950
U.S. EDITION 1949, D. VAN NOSTRAND COMPANY INC.

MADE IN GREAT BRITAIN

PREFACE

THIS study of the British and American constitutional systems was begun while Mr. Harold Stannard was editing a series of pamphlets on current international problems for the Royal Institute of International Affairs, for inclusion in that series. In the course of writing, the author came to the conclusion that the subject merited fuller treatment than could be given in a pamphlet. Hence the present extended essay which Mr. Stannard has described in his introduction as "tentative steps in an almost untrodden field of comparative study." The traditional writing on comparative government, he held, has been too easily satisfied with a juxtaposition of national systems, each treated individually in accordance with its own structural maxims; but the truly comparative character of such studies has been neglected. Moreover, what has been accomplished in recent decades through historical and sociological analysis seemed to call for another effort, on a different level of experience, to clarify the meaning of terms commonly used and all too often abused in public discussion. In this attempt at semantic reduction lies perhaps the greatest value of the present study. Without such attempts, international understanding must be handicapped by misconceptions arising from the inadequacies of linguistic expression.

v

In particular, Britain and the United States still have much to give to each other despite the fact that their relationship is at the present time less evenly balanced through economic circumstances.

Luckily Mr. Stannard was able substantially to complete his manuscript, but he died unexpectedly while making the final revisions. Copious notes left by him have enabled an old-time friend, Mr. John Filmer, to draw on Mr. Stannard's remarkable knowledge in preparing the work for the press. In this task Mr. Filmer has been greatly helped by Professor Henry P. Jordan, of New York University, whose ready help and advice have been accorded at all stages. The editorial collaboration of these two gentlemen, however, did not affect interpretation, which is therefore that of the author.

THE PUBLISHERS.

CONTENTS

BIOGRAPHICAL NOTE

MR. HAROLD STANNARD, whose distinguished academic record at Christ Church, Oxford, included the highest honours in Classical Moderations, *Literae Humaniores* and History, was at the time of his untimely death in December, 1947, a member of the staff of *The Times* in London—a paper with which his association began in 1907. A student of history and politics for upwards of 50 years, he had published a number of studies distinguished by profundity of thought and clarity of style, including a life of Gambetta, "The Fabric of Europe," and "Rome and Her Monuments." His intimate knowledge of European politics led to his employment during the 1914-18 war in the counter-espionage department of Military Intelligence and in the early part of the 1939-45 war as head of the Italian section of the Foreign Relations Press Service of the Foreign Office. A student of colonial questions, he was sent on a mission to the West Indies by the British Council in 1942-43 after serving for some years as a member of the advisory committee on education of the Secretary of State for the Colonies. He had also worked for some years between the wars as a correspondent for the Carnegie Fund for International Peace.

INTRODUCTION

Englishmen take it for granted that foreigners cannot understand their constitution./So largely are its operations dependent on unwritten usage, so subtly and swiftly does it adapt itself to changing circumstances, that only those who have its principles in their blood appreciate its mechanism of checks and balances, and even their reactions to its day-to-day adjustments are inspired rather by feeling than by any conscious intention to maintain or modify its structure./ Knowledge of the American constitution, constructed in one piece and amended by recorded process, is, by comparison, matter of such rational study as lies within the competence of any intelligent and sympathetic mind; so that not only have millions of immigrants become proudly aware of their status as American citizens, but two foreigners, the Frenchman de Tocqueville and the Scotsman Bryce, rank among the authoritative exponents of the constitution's spirit and working. Nevertheless, the constitution could not have kept pace with the vast expansion of the United States except by virtue of its own power of vital growth. In this sense it, too, has its mysteries, revealed only to those who follow the American way of life.

This essay has been written by an Englishman and

therefore must needs exhibit the difference between innate and acquired knowledge. No attempt has been made to conceal it; it may even prove instructive as regards the second of the two purposes that the essay endeavours to serve.

Its first purpose is the satisfaction of intellectual curiosity. How comes it that institutions which admittedly spring from a common root should stand in such sharp contrast to one another? It is argued that for all its sharpness, the contrast is one of means, not of ends nor even of method. In both countries, the end was the combination of public order with individual freedom, and the method of attaining it was to meet the requirements of circumstances. In Britain, circumstances called for a unitary state with the powers of government centralised, and in America for a federal state with the powers of government distributed. The consequences of this difference in circumstances are worked out in detail and it is shown that the English temperament, with its equal insistence on order and on freedom, suffered no sea change when Englishmen crossed the Atlantic. But it is also suggested that the colonists followed an older political tradition than that which had established itself in Britain by the end of the eighteenth century. To remedy the confusion into which England had fallen after the Wars of the Roses, executive power was concentrated in the hands of the Tudor Sovereigns. But in a unitary state such power was unlimited and the sovereignty of the Crown did not lapse with the decease of its wearer. Under such circumstances freedom was lost and order exaggerated into despotism. The passionate assertion of personal rights produced new confusion, which led, under Cromwell, to an attempt to resuscitate the Tudor monarchy with constitutional safeguards. Already, however, a different course of events had been set in train and a solution of the problem was eventually found in the conversion of the Crown into an organ of government acting on the advice of a Committee of Ministers responsible to the elected Chamber. Stress is laid on the kinship in thought between the authors of the Puritan revolution in England and the voyagers in the *Mayflower* who laid the foundations of the American polity, and it is pointed out that the concentration of executive power in one man's hand that in England led straight to despotism became in America a guarantee of freedom, because the power itself was limited and its holder's responsibility to the people was effectively asserted. The writer hopes that these conclusions—tentative steps in an almost untrodden field of comparative study—will prove suggestive to readers on both sides of the Atlantic, will bring home to them the identity of purpose underlying institutions so mutually contradictory in appearance, and help them to realize the essentially indigenous character of their respective systems of government.

In so far as this last aim is achieved the essay will fulfill the second of its two intended purposes. This purpose is eminently practical. Britain and the United States now stand close together in their treatment of international issues and are entirely co-operating in the reconstruction of Germany. The Germans have been singularly unsuccessful in their endeavours to combine order and freedom. In earlier times they often sacrificed order to freedom and endangered the stability of Europe by their weakness. In the late nineteenth and early twentieth centuries, however, they sacrificed freedom to order and threatened the peace of Europe through their strength. Today, under Anglo-American tutelage, Western Germany is bidden rouse itself to another and happier effort. Since Germany has persistently sought unity, even when under Bismarck's leadership its institutions were clothed in federal forms, the American constitutional example has hitherto counted for little in German thought. It counts for very much now and American statesmanship is seeking to adapt it to German conditions. On the other hand, throughout the nineteenth century German liberalism took Britain for its political model and the framers of British policy must now adjust themselves to the fact that they are no longer accepted as the only exponents of true constitutional practice. Given the will for mutual understanding the ways of reaching a solution are manifold. One way—the way of historical comparison adopted in this essay—is to reveal identity of purpose achieved by diversity of means. Other ways, more immediately helpful, maybe, than the elusive pursuit of academic truth, will suggest themselves to other minds, but in the worthiness of aim none can surpass an endeavour to elicit truth not merely for its own invaluable sake but for the furtherance of concord.

CROWN AND CONSTITUTION

IN form and in fact the British and American constitutions are poles apart. So great indeed are their differences that at first glance they defy comparison. In form the American constitution is a document of seven clauses drawn up at Philadelphia in 1787 to which 21 amendments, most of them short, have been added in the course of 150 years. In form the British constitution is an idea existing primarily in the minds of Englishmen, though Scotsmen, Welshmen and Irishmen have helped or hindered them in working it out. In form, too, the United Kingdom is a monarchy and the United States a republic, and these two forms of government are separated from one another in popular thought by the chasm of revolution. In fact—and in politics facts matter more than forms—the British constitution concentrates power in the hands of a Cabinet whose title to govern depends on the confidence of the House of Commons and lapses if that confidence is lost, and the American constitution distributes power among an executive, a legislature and a judiciary, each of which operates of its own right without reliance in the continuing goodwill of either of the others. Equally strik-

ing contrasts may be pointed to in the domestic field
between an omnipotent Parliament and a Congress
whose Acts can be declared null and void by a Supreme Court; in the international field between the in-
definite prerogative of the Crown to conclude treaties
and the provision that entrusts their conclusion to the
President acting by and with the advice and consent
of the Senate; and, permeating the whole field of both
theory and practice, between a federal and a unitary
background.

Yet it is not a stretch of language to speak of both
systems as constitutions, nor an abuse of metaphor
to describe both as springing from the same constitutional root. The authors of the American constitution
were men, English in thought and speech, consciously
working in the tradition that had produced what they
agreed in regarding as the best constitution in the
world; so that one of their essential aims was to provide the United States with a constitution as like as
possible to that of England with the Crown left out.
It is significant that contemporary opinion held them
to have been insufficiently attentive to this aspect of
their work. The first Congress that met under the
provisions of the new constitution promptly added to
it the first ten amendments, which are collectively
known as the Bill of Rights and are a restatement in
suitably modernised terms of the liberties secured to
Englishmen by Magna Carta. The title derives from
the English statute passed in 1689 after the expulsion
of James II.

It is not to be supposed that the authors of the

American constitution were unmindful of those fundamental liberties in defence of which they had repudiated their allegiance and fought a long and difficult
war. If they did not put the reassertion of them in the
forefront of their constitutional proposals, that can
have been only because they addressed themselves
to tasks that they held to be of more urgent necessity.
The delegates who met and talked at Philadelphia
throughout the summer months of 1787 were not
theorists assembled to write on a clean slate the language of their joint political wisdom. Of the three
men who during the tumultuous years of the struggle
for independence had best earned the title of political
philosophers, two—Jefferson and Tom Paine—were in
Europe; the third, Benjamin Franklin, was present,
an honoured and venerable figure, but too patently
near the end of his course to display that fertility in
constructive thought that had distinguished his prime.
The burden of the undertaking successfully carried
through at Philadelphia was shouldered by patriotic
and experienced men of affairs aware that they confronted a crisis. By 1787 the compulsion that had
made of thirteen separate and dissimilar communities
first the United Colonies and eventually the United
States had ceased to operate, and nominal union had
all but degenerated into actual conflict. Some central
government, replacing the authority previously exercised from London, must be instituted if the proud
words "United States" were to retain their meaning,
and it was to this issue, at once immediate and prac-

tical, that the Philadelphia delegates addressed themselves.

In so doing they showed themselves entirely true to
their political ancestry. The English constitution has
evolved and is still evolving over a period of many
centuries because the men who have made it have
never acted except under the pressure of necessity and
have never sought, except perhaps in Cromwellian
times, to go beyond the needs of the moment. Every
landmark in English constitutional history from
Magna Carta in 1215 to the Parliament Act of 1911
is the memorial of a crisis. Only when the normal
friction of political life raises some issue of principle
and involves it in controversy have the English felt
the need of definite language that will put the disputed
principle beyond further challenge; but, once felt,
this need must be satisfied, at best through argument,
at worst by bloodshed. In the same spirit the Americans acquired their independence by war and perpetuated it through debate. The whole relationship of
the British and American constitutions is blurred by
the familiar distinction between the written and the
unwritten. The real distinction is that the one was
written as a whole in a few months and the other has
been written in part during the course of centuries,
and this distinction calls attention to a fundamental
resemblance—the need in both countries of the spur of
necessity to produce the written word.

The reason that the American constitution covers
more ground than any constitutional document in the
English Statute Book and occupies an exceptional and

isolated position to which English history offers no parallel lies in the nature of the crisis that confronted its authors. The Union was breaking up; the Articles of Confederation that had just sufficed to carry it through the war with Britain were visibly failing to maintain it; political dissolution was impending, with symptoms of economic crisis and even a threat of social chaos. If the United States as a political entity was to survive, the terms on which its components were to live with one another had to be defined, and definition meant both a surrender of sovereignty to a new central government and a confirmation of sovereignty to the participating States. The issue of sovereignty is always so vital that once raised it must be finally determined. In England it has been from first to last an issue between the Crown and its subjects, presenting itself under a variety of forms, judicial, financial and religious as well as political, and calling for piecemeal settlement under each of its aspects as they became prominent. But in the United States it arose, as it had not done and could not do in England, in terms of disputes between States, each of which claimed absolute sovereignty in its area. Its form was thus constitutional in the highest and fullest sense of the word, and its settlement called for the erection of a federal structure to serve as a framework or container for all forms of American public life. This was what the Constitution, working of necessity along English lines but going, again of necessity, far beyond English precedents and discarding English practice, was successful in providing.

B

In so far as so profound a divergence can be conveyed by any one word in the common language, the word "convention," in its political significance, sums up the differences between British and American constitutional doctrines. The term belongs to the historical vocabulary of both peoples but carries different meanings to British and to American ears. In Britain a constitutional convention is a matter of usage so well established that it has the force of law; in the United States a constitutional convention is a body of persons specially appointed to draft, amend, ratify or revise a constitution. Thus to all appearances the same word is used to signify two entirely different things; yet in origin the two meanings are historically linked and their divergence is due to historical causes. In both its meanings the term illustrates the influence of the necessity for action upon the political thought of the English-speaking world; but, whereas in England this influence has been felt exceptionally only in times of crisis, its operation in the United States has been so regular and persistent that it has given to the word "convention" a special transatlantic colour.

The clue to the slow constitutional evolution of Britain lies in the permanence of the Crown, which, as the text-books insist, never dies. But though the Crown endures, its wearers do not. Death or rebellion causes them to disappear one by one, and in the formative period of English history each new reign brought up afresh the old question of the relationship of the Crown to its subjects. The English answer to this question was that the relationship must be determined by precedent, and it is characteristic of English practice that every right claimed is alleged to have been exercised in the past—an attitude adopted as clearly in the Parliament Act of 1911 as in Magna Carta of nearly seven centuries earlier. But the appeal to precedent meant not only that the King must conform to the action of his predecessors but also that his own action must be consistent. This latter claim has gone far towards determining the course of English constitutional development. Since all government centres in the Crown it is impossible for the King to discharge all its business himself. But, when once the King had entrusted definite functions to one of his servants, he outraged English conceptions if he either varied or revoked them. What is now called the rule of law and is rightly felt to be the one sure guarantee against governmental oppression was in its origins the maintenance of custom. Through its maintenance, power, though nominally remaining with the Crown, has in practice passed to its servants in such complete measure that even their appointment no longer depends on the Royal will. But the process of transfer has been gradual, a matter of usage hardening into rule. To this process the name of convention has been given, and it is characteristic of the conventions that so largely regulate the operation of the constitution that it is hardly ever possible to point to the exact date on which any one of them became established. When, for example, did the Crown lose its right to veto an Act of the British Parliament? The only possible answer is, that during the first half of the eighteenth century the right gradually atrophied.

Its decay was consequent upon the rise of the party system. So long as the Crown itself chose its executive agents, it could claim to control their proceedings. But when, as a result of the struggles of the seventeenth century, it became clear that the last word on the composition of the ministry rested with Parliament, and when, for the effective use of its powers, Parliament organised itself into parties whose leaders had an irresistible claim on ministerial posts, the Crown found that in practice it had no longer any part to play in the passage of legislation. The fact that the first two Georges were Germans doubtless facilitated the process. Stuart experience had shown what happened to a King who defied Parliament, and the lesson was not likely to be lost on Kings reigning by virtue of a Parliamentary title. When George III, who unlike his two predecessors, was more interested in his British Kingdom than in his Hanoverian Electorate, sought to reassert the powers assigned to the Crown by the Revolution settlement, he recognised that circumstances had changed. Instead of again attempting to draw the rusted weapon of the Royal veto, he sought to control the action of the House of Commons by creating a party of his own—the King's Friends. This was the manoeuvre that the House sought to meet by its resolution, passed in 1780, "that the influence of the Crown has increased and ought to be diminished." The situation did not call for legislation directed against the use of the veto, which in constitutional practice was held to have lapsed, but which remained as a branch of the Prerogative to be called into use again should occasion require.

By the middle of the nineteenth century the occasion had presented itself, and the veto was revived though in a greatly changed form. The grant of self-government to what were then called the Colonies but are now the Dominions brought with it the possibility that the overseas legislatures might pass Acts that directly contravened British legislation or were contrary to British conceptions of public policy. The Royal veto then presented itself as a means of avoiding deadlock, its exercise depending, however, not on the Crown's personal initiative but on the advice of Ministers responsible to the British Parliament. It thus became normal constitutional procedure for a Colonial Governor who was himself appointed on the advice of the Crown's Ministers in London and was answerable for his action to the Secretary of State for the Colonies to "reserve" his assent to Colonial Bills that might create a conflict of jurisdictions.[1] Reservations became less and less frequent as the authority of the

---

[1] In its legislative capacity the Crown still speaks Norman-French—a survival from the days when English was not yet spoken in Court circles. But the King no longer gives the Royal assent in person. A Commission is appointed consisting of the Lord Chancellor and a few senior peers. The formula of assent, pronounced by the Lord Chancellor after the Clerk at the table has read the title of a Bill, is "Le Roi le veult." The formula of rejection is a tactful understatement: "Le Roi S'advisera." A Colonial Governor's action in "reserving" Bills is based on this formula. The Bills are reserved for the consideration of the British Government acting through the Secretary of State for the Colonies.

oversea legislatures increased, and in the Dominions the effective exercise of a veto became impossible after 1926, when the right to advise the Crown on the appointment of a Governor General was transferred from the British to the Dominion Cabinet. Formal repeal of any right of veto was included in the Statute of Westminister, enacted by the British Parliament in 1931, but the provisions of the Statute have not been adopted by all the Dominions.

The special case of Southern Rhodesia illustrates the modern relationship between the abandonment of the veto power and the grant of full self-government. Southern Rhodesia is in transition from Colonial to Dominion status. Its constitution, granted in 1923, has since been several times amended, always in the direction of granting further powers to the local government, whose relations with Britain are now handled by the Commonwealth Relations Office and not by the Colonial Office. But its constitution still contains a clause directing the Governor to reserve Royal assent to a Bill dealing with native policy,[2] and there has

---

[2] "Native policy" is a comparatively new term in English political science and may thus be unfamiliar to American readers. In the early days of European expansion the aim of the Home government was to support the colonists against a sometimes powerful and almost always hostile native population. There are many examples of this in the early history of the thirteen colonies on the American continent that became the original United States. The indigenous inhabitants of the territories thus gradually declined into the category of subject peoples and when their institutions and social structure conflicted with the interests of the colonists they were ruthlessly suppressed. The way of life of the predominantly nomadic and pastoral North American Indians conflicted with the static farming habits of the colonists. The

been public criticism in Britain of the repeated refusal
of the Commonwealth Relations Office to take action
upon Bills so "reserved." On the other hand the veto
power is regularly operative throughout the Colonial
Empire and must necessarily continue to function so
long as the final responsibility for the Government of
the Colonies rests with the British Parliament, even
though the local councils cease to be merely advisory
and are given some degree of legislative sovereignty.
The position was clearly set out early in 1943 when
the then Colonial Secretary offered a constitution to
Jamaica. Its provisions were largely based on proposals submitted by the elected members of the Ja-

colonists, first with the support of the Home government, and
later by their own power and initiative, gradually invaded the
Indian hunting-grounds and when the Indians thus robbed of
the major part of their livelihood resisted, the colonists carried
on a war of attrition against them which ended in the virtual
extermination of the aboriginals. Similar though less extreme examples may be found in the history of other colonies, and, though
there were voices raised against such unethical practices, it is true
to say that those voices had little influence on political thought
until towards the end of last century. Then the idea that a colonial power held its colonial territories in trust for the natives of
those territories began to gain ground in England and received
great impetus from the record of Lord Lugard, to whose doctrine
of indirect rule—that is to say rule of the native population
through their own representatives—the new approach to colonial
policy is largely owing. He conceived his function as Governor
of Nigeria as the representative of the Crown to hold a just balance between the white colonists and the native population. Any
innovation, therefore, likely to disturb unduly the social structure
of the aboriginal population required the careful examination of
the Governor, to be adopted, modified or rejected according to
the prevalent ideas concerning the welfare of the aboriginals.
Thus it has come about that during and since his time a large body
of doctrine has developed that is known in Great Britain as "Native policy."

maican Legislative Council but their claim that the
Governor's power of veto should be abolished or at
least restricted was emphatically turned down. "Under every Colonial constitution without exception,"
wrote the British Colonial Secretary in his despatch,
"when a Bill is presented to the Governor for his
assent on behalf of His Majesty, the Governor has a
discretion to assent, to withhold his assent, or to reserve the Bill for His Majesty's pleasure. Any fetter
expressly imposed by Constitutional instrument upon
this discretion would be without precedent in the
Colonies"; and while agreeing that assent in the King's
name must not be withheld in light-hearted or arbitrary fashion, the despatch refused to agree to "such a
departure in Jamaica from established and universal
constitutional law as would be involved in subjecting
this power, exercisable by the Governor on behalf of
His Majesty, to statutory restrictions."

The history of the Royal veto is thus typical of
the British treatment of constitutional issues. So long
as the responsibility for carrying on the Government
of the country was vested in the King's person, the
King possessed and exercised the right of veto over
legislation that he was not prepared to administer,
though the form in which it was expressed left room
for subsequent discussion. But the constitutional
struggles of the seventeenth century transferred final
authority from the King to Parliament and led by
logical evolution to Government by Ministers responsible to Parliament.

The doctrine of ministerial responsibility was not

clearly established at the time of the Revolution settlement in 1689, but the persistence of the Royal veto
then was due to the special position of King William
III. He was a foreign sovereign married to a British
Princess who stood in the line of succession to the
Crown, but as, rightly enough, he regarded himself
as the head of a Protestant Coalition against Catholic
France, he refused to come to England merely as a
Prince-Consort. The British Parliament saw in him
the necessary preserver of British liberties and therefore offered the Crown to him and his wife jointly on
the terms that the international crisis was felt to demand. So long as William III lived—he survived his
wife and after her death reigned alone—real authority
remained in the Crown. But the position changed
after he had died childless and the Crown had passed
to his wife's younger sister Anne. The Queen could
not head a European coalition and her husband, a
Danish Prince, was a political nonenity. With her,
therefore, authority became transmuted into influence, but that influence was considerable. Pope neatly
summed up her position in the couplet [3]—

And thou, Great Anna, whom three realms obey
Dost sometimes council take and sometimes tea—

and the room in her private apartments, the Queen's
cabinet, has given name to the council over which the
sovereign has ceased to preside. The Queen had her

---

[3] The three realms were England, Scotland and Ireland; the
eighteenth century pronunciation of "tea" still survives in dialect
English.

views and they were respected. Party strength developed rapidly during her life-time, but neither Whigs nor Tories felt able to govern without her support, and it was because her influence had first given all power to the Whigs and had afterwards replaced them by the Tories that her death created a political crisis. Even so, however, she exercised her right of veto only once—in 1706—and by the latter part of her reign she had become aware that she could best get her way by securing a majority in both Houses. Wanting peace with France, she secured it by creating new Peers in sufficient number to change the balance of parties in the House of Lords. Queen Anne was not a woman of marked ability and she had no taste for political intrigue. But she shared the feelings of the average voter of her day, and because her people shared her weariness of the war she was able, without serious opposition, to change the balance of power between parties. But this new position of the Crown as a constitutional make-weight, guiding the swing of the political pendulum between parties and affecting the course of political events by the regular exercise of its influence rather than by the occasional use of its veto-power, could not be maintained after the Queen's death.

The Whigs took immediate and decisive actions to place the Elector of Hanover on the throne. The influence of the Crown, including its right of nomination to salaried appointments that were growing in number and importance with the increase in the country's wealth, was therefore at the unquestioned disposal of the Whigs so long as their Tory rivals were disaffected towards the dynasty and could plausibly be suspected of aiming at a restoration of the Stuarts. In George I's reign the Crown's influence and patronage was in the hands of the party managers. Under George II it came to be exercised in large measure by the Queen, an able and clear-sighted lady who interested herself in English politics much more closely than did her husband and whose firm support of Sir Robert Walpole helped to shift the weight of Parliamentary authority from the Lords to the Commons. Only after 1745, when Prince Charles Edward made his bid for the throne and failed, did it become clear that the position of the dynasty was beyond challenge. On his accession in 1760 George III found, as Queen Anne had found fifty years earlier, a country wearying of a Whig war and a Tory party loyal to the reigning sovereign. In these conditions the King was able to develop the policy of using his patronage, the range of which had now become very wide, to create in the House of Commons a party of his own friends whose votes would swing this way and that according to the Royal direction. The passage in 1780 of Dunning's famous resolution "That the influence of the Crown has increased, is increasing and ought to be diminished" threatened a new breach between King and Commons. The danger was averted, first by Pitt's political genius and the King's mental breakdown, next by the Regent's refusal to aggravate his financial and matrimonial difficulties by embroil-

ment in the party struggle, and finally by the passage
of the Reform Bill in 1832. Yet it is worth remember-
ing that the measure that swept away "pocket" boroughs and turned the House of Commons into a true
reflection of public opinion became law only because
of the King's willingness to create Peers, and that two
years after its passage the King, of his own motion,
dismissed a Ministry. Not until Queen Victoria's
day did the Crown detach itself from party struggles
and though in the later years of her long reign the
Queen did not conceal her partisanship, she remained
faithful to the principles of constitutional monarchy
in which she had been trained, while yet a girl, by
Lord Melbourne. Her attitude made it easy and natural for the Royal veto to be exercised outside the
United Kingdom on ministerial advice when circumstances invited its resuscitation.

Yet so gradual is change under the processes of the
British constitution that the shadow of the veto power
still fell on the political scene throughout George
III's reign and even beyond it. Ministers felt that the
Royal assent might still be more than a matter of form
in the case of a measure that the King could hold to
be a breach of his Coronation Oath, and this consideration long delayed approach to the delicate issue of
Catholic emancipation. To-day the Crown would
probably accept the advice of its Ministers even on
so personal a matter as the interpretation of the Coronation Oath—probably because, with the growth of
its Imperial significance, the Crown has increasingly
sought to avoid entanglement in local controversy,

and its British Ministers have been correspondingly
ready to assume complete responsibility for its action
in domestic affairs. But at critical moments, when
precedent ceases to be an infallible guide, it becomes
impossible to separate the Crown as an institution
from the personality of its wearer. At such moments
the limits of the convention that keeps the Crown out
of politics are reached, and the reigning Sovereign
must himself decide, in the last resort, where his duty
lies. There will be discussions between the King and
his Prime Minister, with whom he stands in specially
close relationship, and the Prime Minister will be fully
acquainted with the King's sentiments before he holds
the Cabinet meetings that will determine the advice to
be formally tendered by the Ministry as a whole. For
such advice Ministers take full responsibility before
Parliament, and personal references to the King in debate are out of order.

The position is well illustrated by the events that
preceded the passage of the Parliament Act of 1911.
Late in 1909 the House of Lords rejected the Budget.
The Liberal Government of the day, regarding this
action as unconstitutional, asked for and obtained a
dissolution. The action of the House of Lords was
the main issue at the ensuing election, and the Government asked for a mandate to curb its powers, but
battle was naturally joined in the constituencies on
the whole record of the Liberal party during its four
years of office. The election confirmed the Government in power, though with a greatly reduced majority, and Ministers brought in their Parliament Bill. It

provided that measures passed by the Commons should become law over the head of the House of Lords—money Bills if not passed by the Lords within a month, other Bills if rejected by the Lords three times in two years. Before the Bill had reached the Lords, King Edward VII died. It was clear that the Bill would not pass the Lords unless the Crown were prepared to create Peers in sufficient number to give the Government a majority and it was felt that the new King should not be called upon to take a decision of such importance within a few weeks of his accession. The leaders of the two parties therefore agreed to confer, and the discussions, which came to cover the whole field of party disagreement, went on for some months. In the end they broke down. Ministers returned to their Bill, and it became necessary to ascertain the King's views. There was a precedent in King William IV's reign for an undertaking, itself founded on the precedent set by Queen Anne, by the King to create as many Peers as were required for the passage of the Reform Bill. To this precedent King George V reverted. He asked, as William IV had asked before him, that he should be left in no doubt as to the will of the people and that they should be consulted again and invited to give, not, as in the previous election, a general mandate for the restriction of the Lord's powers, but a specific mandate for the passage of the Parliament Bill. Accordingly late in 1910 the Parliament elected a few months before was again dissolved. The Government was once more returned to power, with its majority practically unchanged, and Ministers now felt justified in tendering the advice, which the King, for his part, felt justified in accepting, that the Crown's peer-making prerogative should be put at the Government's disposal. Under this threat the Lords passed the Bill, but the King was concerned that his intended action and the motives for it should be made perfectly clear to the House on which he was bringing his coercive powers to bear, and when the initial ministerial statement in debate failed to satisfy him, a second Minister rose later to give a fuller account. So delicate and so personal is the operation, under the British system, of constitutional conventions when employed to resolve a crisis.

In America, on the other hand, there is no King; in his place there is the Constitution; and while the King never dies, the Constitution, being in itself a mere form of words, constantly needs to have the breath of life put into it. This process serves the same purpose and operates with the same motive of ensuring the rule of law as the maintenance of custom (or more strictly convention) in England, and has thus taken over the English name. But the attendant circumstances are utterly diverse. The King who never dies has vanished, leaving a constitutional void to be filled, and the constitutional convention which fills it is one that is called into existence on a specific date for a specific job, and every detail of its progress can be chronologically indicated. The Convention that gave the United States its Constitution began its work at Philadelphia on May 25th, 1787, reached its first vital

decision at the end of that month, came to its crisis when June was passing into July, revised and considerably altered its decisions throughout August, and dissolved on September 17th. The ticking of the clock can be heard right through its proceedings and it can still be heard throughout the processes of the American Constitution. A member of the House of Representatives is elected for two years, a President for four, and a Senator for six. The dates of their elections are fixed by the Constitution, and all the elaborate mechanism of constitutional amendment had to be put in operation a few years ago to enable the interval between a President's election and his assumption of office to be shortened by some weeks.

All American politics are governed by the calendar and American life appears to regulate itself by the constitutional clock. Thus, the history of the World was substantially affected by the fact that 1916 was a Presidential year and 1941 was not, and arrangements which, unless foreign policy remains common ground between parties, will put the United States out of action internationally for about one year in every four have still to be correlated with the march of events. In British politics the calendar does not count. In the last two and a half centuries Parliament has fixed the term of its life first at three years, then at seven, and then at five, and in no case has the term meant very much. The life of a Parliament can always be prolonged by its own legislation or shortened by dissolution. In the British Constitution time does not exist, because the Crown is immortal; in the Amer-

ican Constitution time dominates everything in place
of the evicted Crown. The consequent difference,
both in the structure and in the working of the institutions of the two countries, is enormous, and the
word "convention" has been so stretched to cover it
that its meaning has been broken in two. Historically
the American meaning is the older, and being the
older is necessarily of English origin. An English
parliament can be summoned only by the Crown. It
has, however, happened twice in English history that
there was no Crown to function when a great emergency made the summons of a parliament essential.
The disappearance of the Crown from the scene is
the only occurrence that can throw the constitutional
arrangements of Great Britain completely out of gear,
since they rest upon the assumption that the Crown
never dies. But, first in 1660 and again in 1688, there
was no Crown—in the former year because the Long
Parliament had abolished it and in the latter because
the King had fled the country after wrecking the
machinery of government by throwing the Great
Seal into the Thames.

In these circumstances writs could be issued from
only an unauthorized source. In 1660 they were issued by the Long Parliament itself, which, nominally
of its own motion but actually at the command of the
Army, declared itself dissolved and directed its successor to assemble some six weeks later. In 1688 writs
were issued by the Prince of Orange acting in co-
operation with an *ad hoc* body composed of all the
Privy Councillors in London and all available persons

C

who had sat in any of the Parliaments of Charles II. As a result of the issue of these writs, bodies of elected representatives met in the capital. They were not parliaments because they had not been summoned by the Crown. They were special assemblies and the name "convention" was borrowed for them from ecclesiastical procedure. But as they did the work of parliaments, and as they declared themselves to be as good as parliaments, they are known in English history as convention parliaments. Both dealt with the emergency that had called them into being, the one by restoring the monarchy and the other by defining its powers. The restoration was accomplished once and for all, but as the relations of Crown to parliament were a continuing business the Bill of Rights (1702) passed by the convention parliament of 1689 was re-enacted by its constitutionally summoned successor.

Since the end of the seventeenth century political conditions in England have not made it necessary to call together another convention. But the precedents are available and could be invoked if required, just as the precedent of Queen Anne's special creation of Peers in 1713 to pass the Treaty of Utrecht was invoked to justify a special creation of Peers, should it have proved necessary, by William IV to pass the Reform Bill of 1832. The machinery is there and it is the sort of machinery that does not get rusty for lack of use.

On the other side of the Atlantic the machinery for the summons of a convention was not required until

close to a century after it had ceased to be needed in
England. It was by an extension of the committee
system, originally adopted and developed by English
parliaments of the late sixteenth and early seventeenth
centuries to keep their proceedings secret from the
Crown, that the thirteen Colonies first planned their
rising and began to make contacts with one another.
As the crisis drew on, the Colonies appointed delegates to a central body called the Continental Congress, and this body continued to function after the
independence of the United States had been recognised. Composed, however, as it was of delegates, it
had no real powers, and within a few years it became
clear that if the union was to be maintained some
authority must be called into existence to exercise
functions akin to those previously discharged by the
Crown. The emergency had arisen and the machinery of a convention was set in motion to meet it—of
a convention, however, and not of a convention parliament, because the traditions that the American
colonists had brought with them were those of the
first half of the seventeenth century and knew nothing of the sovereignty of Parliament as established in
1688.

The English tradition thus lay behind the beginnings of the American Constitution. The members
of the Convention were aware of it, and, if they kept
one eye on the Articles of Confederation that they
were nominally revising and on the Constitutions
with which all but two of the thirteen Colonies had
already equipped themselves, they had the other fixed

on English precedent, English models, English methods and English experience.

Accepting tradition as an essential part of his political thought, the Englishman does not trouble to enquire how far his regard for it has affected his institutions; nor does the question admit of an easy answer, because regard for tradition has revealed itself rather in the continuing regulation of his constitutional progress than in the active direction of its development. It is clear, however, that the force of tradition operates against great and sudden changes, and this force is never more active than when substantial change becomes necessary. Of all peoples except the English it may fairly be said that the great steps in their progress are marked by breaks in the established order so abrupt and complete that whether achieved by violent means or not they are deservedly called revolutions. It is, however, a characteristic of revolutions that they get out of hand. Because of the break with the past, control over events is lost. They cease to take their place in the sequence and career off wildly, with the result that a subsequent period of reaction is required to bring them back into the line again. It was in this way that the French Revolution got out of hand after Mirabeau's death and that, but for the eventual victory of Stalin over Trotsky, the Russian Revolution would have got out of hand after Lenin's death. There is only one short period in all the centuries of English constitutional history when events got out of hand, and that was when the Long Parliament took the bit between its teeth and abolished the House of Lords and the Monarchy. The Army sought to apply the curb, and if the Army itself had been under better control it might have given the country a workable written constitution instead of the scrappy improvisations of the Instrument of Government. As things turned out, it was left for Charles II, with his quiet determination not to go on his travels again, to convince the English people in the course of the twenty-five years of his reign that they could not dispense with the Crown and to teach them that when the crisis came in the 1680s they must avoid the errors of the 1650s.

All this was a part of the American inheritance, and the most remarkable feature of the American Revolution was that it did not work itself out to the logical end, later destined to be attained in the South, of the establishment of a number of independent and mutually jealous states. The orderly consolidation of the Colonies on the Atlantic seaboard as a prelude to their immense expansion westward proceeded so smoothly after their repudiation of their allegiance to the King of Great Britain that two of them, Connecticut and Rhode Island, which had the privilege of electing their own governors, did not think it necessary to remodel their constitutions, Rhode Island, indeed, finding it possible to postpone change until as late as 1842. But for the curb of tradition the situation would have got completely out of hand in the ten years following the recognition of independence. The Government in London had dealt with defence, with inter-colonial and oversea trade, and with the regulation of credit and currency. With the repudiation of that Government the various States conducted their own wars with the Indians, put up tariffs against one another, issued local and inconvertible currencies and came to the verge of mutual conflict. The foundations of prosperity were shaken, and a movement in which hopeless debtors combined with unpaid ex-service men filled the business folk of Massachusetts with fears of a social revolution. As Hamilton put it in his rhetorical way when he was commending the results of the Philadelphia Convention to the electors of New York: "What indication is there of national disorder, poverty and insignificance that could befall a community so peculiarly blessed with natural advantages as we are, which does not form a part of the dark catalogue of our public misfortunes?" (*Federalist*, No. 15)

This was the danger that the Philadelphia Convention had to meet, and it met it by playing for time. American writers have admired the restraint of the framers of the Constitution in not attempting to do too much. Their real problem was to do anything. The convention might have failed, and perhaps would have failed, if some of the more extreme delegates, like Patrick Henry, had not failed to put in an appearance at all, or, like Alexander Hamilton, had not prudently withdrawn rather than wreck the prospect of agreement. Even so, John Adams could claim that ratifications of the Constitution had been "extorted by grinding necessity from a reluctant people".

TWICE in her history has England essayed to equip herself with a written constitution and on each occasion the crisis was as universal and as compelling as that which confronted the States of the American Union in 1787. It was, indeed, a crisis of the same kind. In America the central Government exercised by London had disappeared and had to be recreated; in England the King, who was the central Government, had so grievously erred in his understanding and performance of his functions that he had to be replaced. John, it is true, died on the throne and in retrospect the final crisis is seen to have been averted by his acceptance of Magna Carta. But John had repudiated his signature to that great document before a year was out and only his opportune death averted a new rising and a change of dynasty. To Charles I death was less merciful and delayed its coming. Few if any of those who drew up the Petition of Right in 1628 can have anticipated or desired that morning in Whitehall twenty-one years later, and even when the Civil War was lost and the King a captive, events seemed moving to a settlement that would leave him his throne. It was the King himself who kept his tragic course to the end—to the trial of "Charles Stuart" and the last pitiful cry "Remember"—he who would have fared so differently had he known how to forget—while the snow flakes falling in Westminster made the curtain to the grimmest, least desired, yet most inevitable scene in English history.

All Englishmen know that their political liberties

are founded upon Magna Carta though, as the document is written in mediaeval Latin, few of them can confirm their knowledge by a detailed acquaintance with its provisions. However, it is a fact that Magna Carta first established the fundamental political principle of no taxation without representation. As the earliest truly representative Parliament did not meet until 80 years after its signature, its language lacks precision, but it declares that the King is not to impose charges other than the accepted feudal aids without the consent of his common council. Magna Carta also assures even-handed justice according to law. It declares that no free man shall in future be condemned except by the verdict of his peers and the law of the land. Further, in language that established the position of the Crown as the fountain of justice, the King proclaimed that "to no one will we sell, to no one will we refuse or delay, right and justice". Yet, in spite of these far-reaching undertakings, Magna Carta has been depreciated by certain modern critics, partly as a piece of class legislation imposed upon the Crown by the Barons, partly as a mere scrap of paper quickly repudiated by the King and declared by the supreme authority of the Pope to be without binding force. It is true that the position that Magna Carta occupies in the popular mind is largely due to Chief Justice Coke and his fellow seventeenth century jurists who read into it more than it actually contained. It is also true that when Shakespeare put the English historical tradition on to the stage he did not include a Runnymede scene in his "King John", though he

must have realised that it would make excellent thea-
tre. But in politics, if in nothing else, Shakespeare
was strictly of his time and the mere idea of antagonism between Crown and people was obnoxious to
Tudor thought.

Constitutionally, the Tudor period is a diversion
from the main current of English history that, from
Magna Carta onwards, set in the direction of creating
a responsible executive. Throughout the sixteenth
century the mediaeval social order was in dissolution
and the rapid and surprising movement of events
made it essential for the executive to be able to make
decisions without continuously looking back over its
shoulder for Parliamentary support. In Henry VIII's
day, Parliament was not only prepared but anxious
to concentrate power in the hands of the King, even
to the extent of authorising him to regulate the succession to the Crown; and the King, who quite understood that his revolutionary policies would come to
nothing unless he had the nation behind him, did not
hesitate on occasion to reason with Parliament in
order to get his way. Things were not so easy for
Elizabeth. Time and again she sharply reminded Parliament of the limits within which it was competent
to act and she was at pains to keep its sessions short.
But for all her autocratic temper she was her father's
daughter and never allowed herself to antagonise her
faithful Commons. Indeed at the end of her reign,
after the destruction of the Armada had resolved the
crisis, she even yielded with effective oratory, which
has gone down to history as the "Golden Speech," to

a Parliamentary demand for the discontinuance of monopolies.[4] Her Stuart successors had none of her prestige and none of her sensitiveness to public feeling. For Tudor patriotism and Tudor tact they substituted a stiff and exalted conception of Monarchy and thereby quickened the tendency of Parliament to reassert claims long half-heartedly maintained or altogether dormant. In putting them forward appeal was made to the English tradition of liberty as formulated in Magna Carta.

The appeal was reasonable enough. Born of a crisis, Magna Carta occupied a special position in English thought from the time of its signature to the close of the Middle Ages. On King John's death, the guardians of his infant successor, Henry III, reissued it twice, with some modifications, in the next two years. In 1225 the King, now held to be of age, issued it once more over his own signature, in what came to be regarded as the definitive text. Later sovereigns confirmed it, sometimes, if Parliament was suspicious, repeatedly. There are over forty confirmations in the next two centuries. Parliament was equally firm in its attachment to the Charter. More than once it ordered it be read; and at least once, in interesting anticipation of the procedure of the American Su-

---

[4] The granting of monopolies in the manufacture or supply of some article in common demand was Queen Elizabeth's frequent (and cheap) way of rewarding merit, for the recipient received a monetary reward that was paid by the consumer and not by the Queen's treasurer. The great William Byrd, for instance, was given by the Queen the monopoly for the supply of music paper after the completion of his musical setting of the Prayer Book services.

preme Court, it petitioned that all acts that did not square with its provisions be declared null and void. In representing Magna Carta as a fundamental law over-riding all Royal claims, the seventeenth century jurists had good material to work upon.

Nevertheless, Magna Carta is not a notably original document, a mediaeval foreshadowing of the American Constitution. It claims to set out the traditional liberties of Englishmen, giving them precision because they have been violated, and the parallel in American history is not with the original Constitution but with the first ten amendments collectively described, in terms borrowed from England, as the Bill of Rights. Magna Carta's appeal to precedent was deliberate. The Charter was founded on articles presented by the barons to the King, and these articles in turn had their beginning in a conference between the barons and leading ecclesiastics [5] at Bury St. Edmunds in the previous year. At this conference Stephen Langton, Archbishop of Canterbury, produced a charter of Henry I, whose reign had opened more than a century before, and it was on this document that the conference founded its work.

---

[5] The prominence of ecclesiastics in mediaeval councils is illustrated by the fact that the first clause of Magna Carta, recapitulating an undertaking given by the King only a few months before, states that the English Church is to be free. This language does not anticipate the Reformation but means that Cathedral Chapters are to be free in their election of Bishops. By one of the little ironies of history this article is observed in the letter but violated in the spirit. When a See falls vacant, the Crown issues a permit to elect to the Chapter but at the same time names the person to be elected. Full observance of the first clause of Magna Carta would amount to disestablishment.

But the conference went into details where the Norman Kings had dealt in generalities. After the Conquest, William I gave a Charter to London. In English—the original is in Anglo-Saxon, not, it is worth noting, in Norman French—it reads as follows:—

"William, King, greets William, Bishop, and Gosfrith, portreeve, and all the burghers within London, French and English, friendly; and I do you to wit that I will that ye two be worthy of all the laws that ye were worthy of in King Edward's day. And I will that every child be his father's heir, after his father's day. And I will not endure that any man offer any wrong to you. God keep you."

The whole 60 articles of Magna Carta are an expansion of this short document and especially of its penultimate sentence. One clause may serve as an example, the famous 39th clause as done into English and quoted, more than 400 years after its promulgation, in the third article of the Petition of Right addressed by the Commons to Charles I: "By the Statute called 'The Great Charter of the Liberties of England'" (the reference is to the definitive re-issue by Henry III in 1225) "it is declared and enacted that no freeman may be taken or imprisoned or be disseised of his freeholds or liberties, or his free customs, or be outlawed or exiled or in any manner destroyed, but by the lawful judgment of his peers or by the law of the land". (Modern translators would substitute "and" for "or" in the closing phrase). Here is that clear conception of justice as the safeguard of liberty that has meant so much in English political thought; the very language of the clause is echoed in the constitutions of some of the States of the American Union, and its spirit dictated the fifth and sixth amendments to the Constitution of the United States. Further, the definition, in other clauses of the Charter, of the rights that the 39th Clause entrusts to the protection of the Courts is the first clear example of that accurate, matter-of-fact thinking about political matters that in the American Constitution finds its most striking example in the section of Article I that defines the powers of Congress.

If Magna Carta was not original in its statements, it broke entirely new ground by attaching a sanction to its provisions. Its 60th and final clause empowers the barons to elect 25 of their number, with a standing committee of four to keep a strict eye upon the due observance of the King's undertakings, who are authorised to rebel and to proceed to any lengths short of the actual seizure of the King and his family should he not keep his word. This is the first approach to the problem, central in English history, of imposing responsibility on the executive. It offered the only solution possible at the time, for the King had lately made his peace with the Church and the baronage was the only power capable of putting pressure upon him. In view of the restrictions placed on the King's right to tax, the absence of any reference to Parliament may cause surprise. But Parliament was still in process of gestation—it did not become a normal working part of the constitutional machinery until the reign of John's great-great-grandson, Edward III—and the power of the purse was still unrealised. Magna Carta thus chose the one possible agency of compulsion, but it has proved a part of England's good fortune that its choice proved abortive because it ran counter to the tradition which placed sovereignty in the Crown. Otherwise the country might have experienced such a period of feudal anarchy as it had not known since Stephen's reign.

If Magna Carta only reasserted tradition when it was effective, and proved ineffective where it tried to establish a new form of Government, what is the explanation of the special reference that attaches to it? Four circumstances combined to give Magna Carta its unique status. First and foremost, it was not, like earlier Charters, granted by the King of his good pleasure and therefore revocable by him and not binding upon his successors. Its terms were dictated to the Crown by its subjects. In the idiom of a later date the Charter was a Social Contract. Secondly, the gravity of the crisis—for the realm would fall to pieces if the King did not duly discharge the obligations of his office—led to an unprecedented combination of forces. Not only were the leading ecclesiastics associated with the barons at Runnymede, but representatives of the towns were also present. The estates of the realm were beginning to merge into the English nation. Next, the Charter was exceptionally comprehensive in its terms, applying to all free men, not to privileged groups. Lastly, the proposed sanction, ineffective though it proved, laid down the principle that the Crown itself was subject to law and that, if need were, force could and would be applied to compel it to recognise its position. There had been nothing like this in English history before; there was to be nothing like it again. The circumstances attending the signature of Magna Carta justify the view, dear to English thought, that it ranks as a fundamental law, and its position in men's minds gives it, in fact, just such an immunity from change by ordinary legislative procedure as is bestowed by formal enactment upon the Constitution of the United States.

It was in the middle of the seventeenth century, during the brief term of the Protectorate, that the line of English constitutional development came near to switching on to that eventually traced out by the members of the Philadelphia Convention. Nothing else was to be expected. The men who governed England in the 1650s were the contemporaries of the Pilgrim Fathers whose example and precept have done so much to shape the American way of life; and this real parallel in mental attitude is enhanced by an apparent parallel in circumstances. On the face of it the same problem perplexed constitutional statesmanship in seventeenth century London and in eighteenth century Philadelphia—that of maintaining British institutions while leaving the King out. But in America the King had gone, and had gone the more completely because he had never been present except in the person of his numerous changing representatives, whereas in England the King was merely on his travels, his

eventual return from which had been rendered probable by the horror aroused among the people by the
means adopted to rid the country of his father. On
the other hand, the federal issue that overshadowed
everything else at Philadelphia hardly presented itself to the minds of Cromwell and his councillors.
True, the Government in London, being an English
Government, felt the need of regulating its relations
with Scotland and Ireland and went so far as to nego-
tiate with the Scots. But when, in 1653, an attempt
was made to put the rule of the Army on a legal
foundation, the fate of both countries was settled in
summary fashion. In December of that year Britain
was given a constitution—the only written constitution it has ever known—and the opening words of
that document declared both Scotland and Ireland to
be incorporated in the Commonwealth. A very different temper necessarily prevailed at Philadelphia,
where all prospect of maintaining the Union was
rightly felt to depend on a fair and lasting distribution
of authority between the new central government and
the thirteen sovereign States. All the emphasis of the
American Constitution falls on its federal character;
all the emphasis of the Instrument of Government,
the name given by the Cromwellian army to the constitution that it produced, falls on the person who
replaced the King.

Historical study has intensified that emphasis.
Cromwell's temper and policy have left their mark
upon England, but the institutions through which he
chose, or was compelled, to govern were evanescent.

Accordingly the interest of later generations has fastened on the Protector himself rather than on the institutions of the Protectorate, and neither the Instrument of Government nor its later modifications occupy much space in English textbooks.[6] It may be that fuller consideration of the steps that England once took in anticipation of the American approach to constitutional settlement, and of the reasons for the failure in one country of a method that was later so successful in the other, would contribute towards a good understanding between the two peoples.

As will be seen, the American Constitution and the Cromwellian Instrument of Government have a good deal more in common than the fact that both were completely shaped and given the permanence of written record by the bodies that created them. They differ, however, in one all-important respect. Whereas the Americans were above all things at pains to perpetuate the Union by devising arrangements that promised to endure, their English predecessors became more and more conscious that they were merely providing for an interregnum. The tone of the Instrument of Government is, indeed, authoritative and final. Like Magna Carta it is imposed from without, though Cromwell as Captain-General must have had an important say in its provisions, and like Magna Carta it offers no machinery for its subsequent modi-

---

[6] There are at least two references to Cromwell in each of the twelve pages (420-431) which Trevelyan in his *History of England* devotes to the Protectorate; but the Instrument of Government is not mentioned.

D

fication. But when a Parliament met under the terms
of the Instrument, it promptly (1654) recast it in the
form of a Constitutional Bill, with changes reasserting
Parliamentary sovereignty. Already power in England was beginning to shift from the Army, functioning through its Captain-General, to the House of
Commons legislating in partnership with an individual whose constitutional place differed from that of
the King both in its title and in the limits imposed on
its authority. Three years later, however, the limits
have almost faded out. In 1657 Parliament put forward proposals for constitutional change. They were
addressed to the Lord Protector in the form of a
Humble Petition and Advice—terms in which Parliament might have addressed the Sovereign of a generation before. Evidently England was slipping back
into her traditional ways and it only remained to
complete the process by scrapping the new-fangled-
title of Lord Protector and restoring the august and
familiar monosyllable, King.

History is full of might-have-beens, and it is indeed
tempting to speculate on the probable course of constitutional events in England had Cromwell's life
been prolonged for another five years—years during
which account must needs have been taken of a ma-
ture and active claimant to the Throne. With his
realistic mind, Cromwell was fully aware of the
growing hold of the monarchial tradition upon English opinion. He had himself moved with the times,
and his signature had changed from Oliver Cromwell
to Oliver P. (Washington, who realised how closely

he had moved in Cromwell's footsteps, was too good
a Republican to imitate him in this respect). It may
be that as the monarchial trend became more emphatic, Oliver P. would have given place to Oliver R.[7]
In that case the King, first sovereign of a national
dynasty, would have anticipated George III by just a
century. Or it may be that, recognising the immense
strength of a legal title, Cromwell would have come to
terms with the exiled Prince and become the First
Minister of a restored King. In that case he would
have anticipated the younger Pitt by basing his authority in the State on something other than the Royal
favour. But history seldom takes short cuts, preferring roundabout and painful roads to compromises
suggested by reason at the outset before the passions
are roused. Cromwell left the main constitutional
issue unresolved and his death faced the country with
the naked choice between a Restoration and a renewal
of civil war. In the Declaration of Breda (April
1660), the document that assured the King's recall
from his travel by its promise of political, religious
and economic peace, Charles II could refer to the
restoration not only of the monarchy—the sense in
which the term is used nowadays—but of "King,

---

[7] Kings sign by their Christian names followed by "R"—the
initial letter of the Latin word "Rex," King. Cromwell went half-
way towards the monarchical signature when he dropped his
surname, but in place of "R" wrote "P"—the initial letter of Protector in both Latin and English. In making his choice he could
hardly have failed to remember that a Prince of Wales signs by
his Christian name followed by "P" for Princeps, Mediaeval Latin
for Prince; so that his "P" when read by monarchist eyes placed
him at but one remove from the Crown.

Peers and people to their just, ancient and fundamental rights". The wheel had indeed come full circle and the English experiment in republicanism was at an end.

In its course, however, it had presented resemblances to, and differences from, the provisions of the American Constitution that are worth noting, although the resemblances so quickly weakened and the differences increased. The English Constitution professed to have settled without difficulty the question that gave so much trouble to the members of the Philadelphia Convention, whether power should be vested in an individual or in a governing body. The supreme legislative authority "of the Commonwealth", declared the Instrument of Government in its first clause, "shall be and reside in one person and the people assembled in Parliament", and the Parliamentary Bill echoed this language. It implied that the Lord Protector had a right both to initiate and to veto legislation. The American Constitution limits the right of initiation. A President cannot introduce a Bill into Congress though he can send a message advising its introduction, and in practice Bills often are introduced, though they seldom are passed in the form desired, by the administrative department concerned. On the other hand, the President has a more effective right of veto than that conceded to the Lord Protector by the Instrument of Government. Congress requires a two-thirds vote to pass a Bill over the veto, but the Instrument of Government laid it down that in case the Lord Protector "shall not give his consent"

to Bills "within twenty days after they shall be presented to him, or give satisfaction to the Parliament"
(that is, obtain Parliamentary approval of his objec-
tions) "within the time limited . . . that then such
Bill shall pass into and become law although he shall
not give his consent thereunto". The Parliamentary
Bill, however, restored to the Protector an absolute
right of veto on any Bill "to alter the foundation and
constitution of the Government of this Commonwealth from a single person and a Parliament"—the
only example in English history of a process of constitutional amendment different from that of ordinary
legislation and as such foreshadowing the more elaborate distinction drawn in the Constitution of the
United States.

The principle of the separation of powers, which
the eighteenth century felt to be of fundamental importance, did not commend itself to seventeenth century needs and the second clause of the Instrument of
Government declared "that the exercise of the chief
magistracy and the administration of the Government
. . . shall be in the Lord Protector, assisted with a Council, the number whereof shall not exceed twenty-one
nor be less than thirteen". A later clause (25) appointed fifteen members of this Council and provided
that on a vacancy occurring Parliament should nominate six suitable candidates, from whom the Council,
by a majority vote, should select two, leaving the final
choice to the Lord Protector. The American Constitution makes no provision for a Council or for a
Cabinet, which is what the Council eventually be-

came, but the conciliar idea was not absent from the minds of the Framing Fathers. In particular it was their intention that the Senate should be associated with the President in the conduct of international affairs, though the actual language and subsequent practice of the Constitution does not go beyond requiring the consent of the Senate, by a two-thirds vote of those present, to the conclusion of treaties. The Instrument of Government naturally goes further than this and declares that the Lord Protector shall "with the consent of the major part of the Council, have the power of war and peace".

The office of Lord Protector like that of President was made elective, though its term was limited only by the death of its holder, and the Instrument of Government vested the election of a new Protector in the Council. No constitutional detail caused so protracted a difficulty at Philadelphia as the method of electing a President and the procedure eventually devised has hardly ever worked as intended. Difficulties would have arisen in England, too, had the Protectorate endured, for when Parliament considered the Instrument of Government, it promptly attacked the wide authority of the Council and particularly its power of electing the Protector. According to the Constitutional Bill (November 1654), "the manner of electing the Protector, in the vacancy of a Protector (sitting the Parliament) shall be such as the Parliament shall think fit", but the Council retained its power if Parliament was not in session. In the Humble Petition and Advice (May 1657), however,

Parliament proposed to abdicate its functions and to leave to the Lord Protector, as it had left to Henry VIII, the nomination of his successor; so powerfully were events moving towards a re-creation of the constitutional position of the Tudor monarchy. Parliament had, further, in 1654, sought to deprive the Council of all voice in the filling of vacancies in its membership, proposing instead "that the persons who shall be of the Council shall be such as shall be nominated by the said Lord Protector and approved by the Parliament". No less significantly Parliament was not prepared to leave the Council its voice in the declaration of war; "the power of making war is only in the Lord Protector and the Parliament" (clause 52).

The Instrument of Government was at pains to make Parliamentary legislation a reality and therefore provided for the summons of Parliament "once in every third year", with provision against its premature dissolution. The Constitutional Bill amplified these arrangements by introducing the calendar into English politics. It provided that a new Parliament should "meet and sit at Westminster the third Monday of October 1656", its successor "upon the third Monday in October 1659, and so likewise on the third Monday in October in every third year successively". Power was also given to the Lord Protector to call Parliament together "when the necessities of State shall require". To all these arrangements there are close parallels in the American Constitution, as there are to provisions vesting the command of the country's armed forces in the Lord Protector.

The Englishman reading the constitutional documents of the Protectorate will find in them much that anticipates what is now familiar usage, notably the distinction between the King in Parliament and the King in Council,[8] and will note in the proposal that nominations to the Council shall be subject to Parliamentary approval—the germ of the doctrine of Cabinet responsibility. The American, in a similar reading, will find himself at home with documents that cover the whole constitutional field and are precise in their attribution of powers. It is in these documents, in fact, that the English and American streams of constitutional thought find their meeting place, and for this reason they have a value in the comparison of the two constitutions out of all proportion to their practical significance in history.

The differences between the two constitutions leap to the eye; it could not be otherwise in view of the

---

[8] That formal distinction is of course much older, but until the Tudors there was no practical difference between the King in Council and the King in Parliament. Henry VII began the practice of giving his confidence to men of ability, hardly ever great nobles, who sat in the House of Commons and guided debate there in the way the King wanted it to go. These were the Privy Councillors—the executive as opposed to the legislature. By this device the Tudors secured Parliamentary sanction for all their acts, and had at the same time a small and manageable body of adivsers in place of the mediaeval Kings' Great Council, which was Parliament itself. When the Stuarts thought that they had thus found in the Privy Council the means to govern the country as an absolute monarchy, Parliament as a whole and the House of Commons in particular became simply an opposition. It was to overcome this conflict, which had developed steadily after the death of Queen Elizabeth, that the specific clause in the Instrument of Government was drafted.

different circumstances with which the constitution-makers had to deal. The problem before the Philadelphia Convention was to create a Central Government capable of holding the thirteen States together, and so urgent was the need to solve it that the one issue left, if not open, at least not definitely closed, eventually led to the Civil War. Viewing their task in its true perspective, the Framing Fathers were less concerned to work out the relations of the parts of the Central Government to one another. Enough to lay down the principle of the separation of powers. In England this principle was inapplicable, all powers being centred in the Crown, and would in any case have been inadequate because the King was always there, whereas in America he had been represented only by Governors who came and went. Hence the problem of establishing a responsible executive, which has been central to English constitutional development, could in America be disposed of by making a Governor owe his position to the choice of the people instead of the pleasure of the Sovereign, and this method was already well established when it was also applied to the election of a President. But it is important to note that the English did not begin to find their way towards the democratic solution of their problem until just before the American Constitution was drafted. Pitt's device of appealing to the country, not in order to get a majority of King's friends who would support him, but in order to give a firm basis to his authority after the King's support had enabled him to wear down the opposition in the House of

Commons, is as much a constitutional landmark on one side of the Atlantic as was the assembly of the Philadelphia Convention on the other. It follows that the two constitutions do not admit of any close comparison during the century and a half in which they have been running their parallel courses and, in particular, that it is futile to represent either constitution as superior to the other. They were dealing with entirely different circumstances and therefore adopted entirely different methods. But because both constitutions were the work of men who thought in the same sort of way because they had the same intellectual background, the differences between them occasion surprise, so that when either Englishmen or Americans first become acquainted with the others' institutions they are disposed to criticise them as outlandish and perverse. The reaction is the stronger because, given the mental attitude rightly assumed to be common, the institutions appear to develop naturally out of the circumstances. So indeed they do; but the circumstances are altogether different, and the interest of the comparison lies in tracing out the effect of their differences on action.

There emerges, in the end, an awareness of resemblances, deep-seated but fundamental—but resemblances of modes of political thought, not of forms of political organisation. Time is not likely to lessen these formal divergences. There is no federal problem for Britain, least of all in her relations with the Dominions. Geography brought the States of the American Union together and compelled them to

accept a common superior authority; geography keeps
Britain and the Dominions apart and compels each of
them to require the assurance of full liberty of action.
In these circumstances Ireland, not geographically one
with Britain but not remote enough to be entirely
apart from her, offers constitutional riddles to which
an answer has still to be found. Conversely America
has never had to face the problem of executive responsibility. Urgent when the executive authority
holds his position for life, it becomes of minor importance when he is elected every four years. It indeed
may be contended that one aspect of that problem,
the relation of the executive to the legislature, has
been examined with greater thoroughness and over a
much longer period in Britain than in the United
States; it may even be prophesied that, with the defiance of the convention which forbade a President to
hold office for more than two terms, this question will
become increasingly important in American politics.
Even so, however, the British solution by the ultimate
subordination of the Cabinet to Parliament cannot be
adopted. No Congress, be it ever so perfect a representation of democracy, can claim to dominate a
President whose title to democratic authority is as
good as its own.

In these vital matters the two constitutions, having
diverged at the start, will continue to diverge as each
pursues its own line of development. For that very
reason special interest attaches to the occasions when
the two lines come within sight of one another. The
approach to coincidence was naturally greatest during

England's one experiment in republicanism, and it is curious that the records of the Philadelphia Convention do not include a single reference to the Instrument of Government, though its members explored the history of classical antiquity for precedents to guide them. Other parallels can be drawn that are of value as indicating the causes of the fundamental identity of the two peoples in outlook but that are too remote in date to have any bearing on their institutions. Thus emigrants from all the countries of Europe were impressed with their common American quality by the century-long conflict with untamed nature involved in the conquest of the frontier. Similarly Norman lord and Saxon villein were welded together and became Englishmen during the generations in which they laboured side by side at clearing the forests and draining swamps. But the circumstances of the eleventh and the nineteenth centuries differed too widely for common experiences to have had similar political effects.

There is greater temptation to stress the parallels between the American Constitution and the Tudor monarchy. The Tudor system was born of a crisis and, as was becoming clear in the closing years of Elizabeth's reign, could not endure when the crisis was past. The American Constitution was also born of a crisis and, as Lincoln so clearly realised, must endure if the crisis is not immediately to recur. Both systems established a strong executive and in so doing effected a real separation of powers. The fact is veiled in Tudor England owing to the unifying authority of the Crown during the many years that the crisis, at first mainly religious and later mainly political, was at its height; but in fact, Crown, Lords and Commons were each sovereign in their respective spheres, and none of the three had any constitutional means of over-riding or coercing the other two. Only parallel circumstances are required to make the latent resemblances of English and American ideas about government flare up into prominence, and there was in fact an instructive similarity between the situation that had caused the Philadelphia Convention to assemble and that which confronted Elizabeth at the beginning of her reign. The Queen was faced with religious chaos much as the Convention was faced with economic collapse, and her Acts of Supremacy and Uniformity offered the minimum settlement that the circumstances demanded. She used her new Acts with discretion, preferring, for example, not to demand the oath of supremacy from the judges. Her main purpose in passing them was to gain time. If only the lines of her settlement could have time to harden before the inevitable clash with Spain, then England would be safe; this is the thought that gives the clue to all her twists and prevarications during the next thirty years. So, too, the authors of the Constitution were satisfied that their proposals represented the minimum foundation for their country's future development, and that if the new institutions were only given time to take root the United States could assuredly go forward to the manifest destiny to which her people were already aspiring. They could not,

indeed, foresee that before twenty years had passed
the new Republic would be in danger of being en-
gulfed in the great European struggle, though Washington foresaw it clearly enough a decade later when
he commended isolationism to his country. But they
could foresee that sooner or later there must come a
clash between the States that abominated slavery and
the States that based their whole economy upon it.
The Convention had quickly realised that it could not
settle this critical issue. The utmost that it felt able
to do was to postpone for twenty years the question
of the slave traffic, a question that would clearly prove
the skirmishing ground prior to an attack on slavery
itself. Here, too, the Convention sought to gain time
whose influence was not allowed merely to direct the
operation of the Constitution but, in this grave matter,
was extended to cover the promise of its continued
existence; and it was with this time factor in mind
that Hamilton drove so strongly ahead with his programme for buttressing the new federal institutions
with a strong federal administration, that thirty years
after the Constitution came into force the Federalist
Party which he created was falling to pieces because
it had attained all its cbjectives.

By then, however, time had done its work and the
Constitution was firmly established, in spite of the
jolt given it when the House of Representatives
rushed the Executive into the war of 1812. The Constitution was working, the prosperity of America was
visibly rising, the great expansion westward had begun, the first new States, Kentucky and Tennessee,

having been admitted into the Union before the eighteenth century was out. When Americans of the
1820s looked back on conditions of the 1780s, a period
well within living memory, they were filled with a
natural and overwhelming gratitude to the men who
had devised remedies for the evils that had been so
urgent and with an equally natural and overwhelming
admiration for the institutions to whose operation they
felt they owed their present good fortune. This was
the beginning of that uncritical worship of the Constitution—not unlike the temper in which Englishmen
look back on their Elizabethan glories—that charac-
terised American political thought until the Civil War
and even after. Actually the Constitution underwent
a fundamental change during this period. Before 1830
democracy had broken the barriers erected against it,
and the careful safeguards intended to surround the
election of a President had proved inoperative. But in
form the Constitution remained almost unaltered.
What was even more important, it was functioning
substantially as its authors intended it to function. It
was providing the minimum of authority required to
hold the country together and it was giving full scope
to the initiative both of the States and of individuals.
During this period, as again in the halcyon years after
the Civil War, the executive, except during the
stormy interlude of Andrew Jackson's presidency,
was content to make itself subordinate to the legislature, and in the legislature there was, during this earlier phase of congressional government, no doubt
about the superiority of the Senate. Never since has

its fame stood so high as in the 1830s and 1840s, and it must be remembered that the Senate is a body in which every State is equally represented so that its supremacy was proof that the States were the predominant element in the Constitution and that the fears of an earlier generation that State powers would wither under the blight of the central authority had proved unfounded.

In the second generation of the Constitution's life, as in the first, time was allowed to do its work. When de Tocqueville wrote his *Democracy in America*, which was published in 1835, there was no hint of irony about his title. Democracy was what he found, and as he was more interested in results than in origins, it did not concern him that a common resolve to avert the danger of democratic excesses was what had principally kept the Philadelphia Convention together. So admirably did the political framework that they devised correspond to the requirements of an expanding and developing community that it could accomodate itself to a transformation of the spirit within it; and when the crisis came in 1860 no American on either side really doubted that the country's institutions were suited to the genius of the people, though there was room for passionate dispute about the meaning of those institutions in the last resort. When the Southern States seceded and set up their separate Confederation, the Constitution that they gave themselves differed surprisingly little from that drawn up at Philadelphia seventy years earlier. After the Civil War the development of the United

States was resumed with renewed impetus, and the Constitution naturally received its share of the credit for America's wonderful progress in the last third of the nineteenth century. A more skeptical temper appears to prevail now. It is not unconnected with the shift of the majority of the population from the countryside to the towns, and with the new social problems which such transfer necessarily involves. But the Constitution faces the problems of the modern world with a hundred-year tradition of its own behind it, and behind that again lies, as has been pointed out, the long tradition of the means of ensuring constitutional liberty in England.

There is, therefore, nothing paradoxical in the suggestion that the Constitution of the United States commands from Americans just that sort of affectionate reverence that Englishmen feel towards the Crown. It is not only that the Constitution took over the functions of the Crown when the Crown's authority was repudiated. It is that the whole political experience of Americans has centred round their relations with the Constitution in the same way as the political experience of Englishmen has centred round the Crown. Nor is it an accident that, just as the powers of the Crown were the cause of the one great struggle that has caused Englishmen to fight one another, so the meaning of the Constitution was at issue in the parallel and more terrible struggle in the United States. In both countries national feeling needs a rallying point, something fixed and stable in a world of change, and whereas in England that point is found in a person whose powers have been defined and regulated in the course of centuries, so in America it is found in a document in which the powers of government in general have been defined and regulated once and for all.

II

KING, PRESIDENT, PRIME MINISTER

KINGSHIP as introduced into England by the Saxon invaders was an elective institution. The Saxon King was the leader of his people in peace and war, particularly in war, and a certain Teutonic quality that Tacitus noted nearly nineteen hundred years ago in his book on Germany made the people obey as freemen and not as slaves and caused them to insist upon their own choice of the leader into whose keeping they were entrusting their lives. In this rudimentary form, at the outset of their political development, the ancestors of the English realised and applied the great truth that for all time to come was to guide the political sense of their descendants, that government is by the consent of the governed.

Two considerations, however, tended to restrict the field of choice of a King. One was that a man capable of governing was most likely to be found in the circles with experience of government; the other, which became more important as the Saxon community settled down and the King was less likely to die in battle, was that a reigning King was particularly qualified to indicate his successor. It was this consideration that caused the death-bed nomination of Edward the Confessor to count for so much when the direct line failed with him, just as it was the former consideration which gradually restricted kingship in England to members of the House of Cerdic, to which all wearers of the English Crown except Harold and the first four Norman Kings have in fact belonged since English history became coherent. Yet, as the choice of Harold proved, it was still possible in the eleventh century to go outside the reigning House when emergency demanded, and, as the choice of William Rufus proved, kingship inside the reigning House did not necessarily descend to the eldest son.

A change in the basis of kingly rule was, however, introduced by the Normans when, by the mere fact of their effective conquest of England and by the definite forms of feudalism that they introduced, governorship was intimately associated with the possession of land. By feudal rules, however, land passed from father to eldest son, this being the surest means of keeping fiefs intact and of avoiding disputed successions. The King was a great land owner and on the face of it there seemed no clear reason why a rule that governed the ownership of land in the case of subjects should not also apply to the monarchy. The transition from leadership in action to territorial sovereignty was complete by King John's time. He is the first English King who styles himself *Rex Angliae* (King of England) and not *Rex Anglorum* (King of the English), and it so happens that he is the first English

King to be succeeded by his eldest son when that son was still a boy.

The case of Henry III is, however, by no means clear. Only a little while before his death King John had received his Kingdom back as a fief from the Pope, and directly after his death his nine-year-old heir was hastily crowned either by, or at the suggestion of, the Papal Legate. The situation had called for swift action. John had again antagonised his barons. The French King was actually in England and was preparing to claim the Crown, and the Papal Legate's action was the only means of maintaining the dynasty. The first King who succeeded in childhood by indubitable hereditary right was Edward III's grandson, Richard II, and it has been suggested that had the same situation arisen a century earlier the boy King would probably have been passed over in favour of his experienced uncle, John of Gaunt. After Richard II's deposition Henry IV, who was not the senior member of his branch, hastened to fortify his claim by a parliamentary title, Parliament having by now become the acknowledged mouthpiece of the people and therefore the proper agency of election. When, however, the Yorkists displaced the Lancastrians, they based their title entirely on hereditary right, and the helpless Parliament was forced to declare that the Lancastrians had been usurpers. After Bosworth, Henry VII, like Henry IV, sought Parliamentary backing for his claim, though at the same time he strengthened it by his marriage with the Yorkist heiress. Parliament, however, warned by its experience in Yorkists times, was in no mood to assert its right to regulate the succession by constituting itself an electoral body, and when in Henry VIII's day the demise of the Crown [1] had again become uncertain, it passed an Act empowering the King to settle the succession in his will. Here, and here only, the electoral principle ceases to affect the British Monarchy, but, having been dislodged from the constitution in one critical period, it was restored in another, and more than any sovereign since Saxon times Charles II owed his throne to the free and undoubted choice of his people. By the end of the seventeenth century Parliament's claim as the body representing the electors of the realm to determine the succession was explicitly asserted in the Act of Settlement.

What one parliament has done another parliament can undo, at any rate in theory; and the order of succession to the Crown was in fact modified by Act of Parliament as recently as 1936.[2] The old elective principle has never completely disappeared. The first act of a new King is to meet the members of his Privy Council, reinforced for the occasion, it is interesting to note, by the Lord Mayor of London, to inform them he is ascending the Throne. Moreover, the Coronation service opens with the four-fold pres-

[1] "Demise of the Crown" is in British constitutional usage, the form of words that indicate the transmission of the Crown from one wearer to another. The old sense of the word "demise," obsolete in other contexts, is maintained in this phrase, which is still current. It was used by King Edward VII in his first speech from the Throne in 1901 and occurs in the Act of 1936 by which Parliament accepted the abdication of King Edward VIII.
[2] In "His Majesty's Declaration of Abdication Act."

entation of the Sovereign as "the undoubted King of this realm," and his acclamation by the congregation assembled in the Abbey; and it must not be forgotten that for many centuries coronation followed promptly upon ascension, as it does to this day in the case of Popes, who are also elected sovereigns.

AGAIN and again in the course of American history it appears that action has been taken in accordance with the traditions that the colonists brought with them, and that traditions which, through conventions made valid by time, have become obsolete in the Mother Country have developed new vigour and produced new consequences on the other side of the Atlantic.

It is therefore of some importance to determine just what traditions the American colonists brought with them. Only one colony, Virginia, had been established before relations between Crown and Parliament became seriously embarrassed. The large emigration that colonised Massachusetts and the States of Rhode Island, Connecticut and New Hampshire, which were originally offshoots from it, took place between 1620 and 1640. The powers of the Crown, and especially those powers that it claimed as a matter of divine hereditary right, were now contested, and the emigrants, loyal subjects of the King though the Pilgrim Fathers might proclaim themselves, were by temperament Parliament men. Between 1640 and 1660 emigration practically ceased, but after 1660

Charles II opened up large areas for settlement by granting them to proprietors, and during the next twenty-five years a body of members of the land-owning class crossed the Atlantic and renewed in Virginia and the Carolinas what had now become their traditional way of life. These settlers were King's men, but with all the qualifications that the Restoration settlement had introduced into the meaning of that once sweeping word. They were out of sympathy with the high prerogative claims of James II. They did not go so far as the Parliament men of an earlier generation who had felt themselves entitled not merely to depose but to execute a King, but they held, with the House of Lords of their own day, that a King by misconduct could render the throne vacant. Only one colony, Georgia, was founded after 1688, but as the purpose of its foundation was philan-throphic, and as it was originally colonised by people who had made a mess of their lives in the Old World, it made no signficant new contribution to American thought.

There was thus a double tradition running through American life during the eighteenth century. On the one hand there was the tradition of Massachusetts, which held that government was by the consent of the governed to the extent that the people could put Kings up and pull them down, and this was the tradi-tion which, when events evoked it, came to expression in rebellion. There was also the Southern or Cavalier tradition, which cherished a preference for monarchy as an institution but held that it was the business of the King of an English country to agree with his local parliament. Because circumstances brought both traditions into activity, the rebellion covered all thirteen colonies and was not limited to the Northern group. But because the two traditions were not and could not be completely fused, a large body of American colonists eventually migrated to the maritime provinces of Canada, while the descendants of those Southerners who remained behind repudiated the Northern claims at the time of the Civil War on what was fundamentally the same issue of local as opposed to central sovereignty.

It is in this setting that the proceedings of the Philadelphia Convention on the vital matter of the executive can properly be placed. Settlement was no easy business. There were thirty divisions on this one issue during the proceedings of the Convention, and the compromise eventually accepted was only arrived at in the third month of its sessions. The King had gone, and with him had gone the controls that he had exercised. Events had shown that in some form or other these controls needed to be reinstated, and the Virginian plan with which the Convention had begun its work demanded the creation of an effective executive but left it open whether it should consist of one person or of several. Working on this question, Hamilton actually proposed the creation of a President and a Council all of whom were to be appointed for life and empowered to nominate the State governors. This was to revive on American soil and in a very different atmosphere the Mediaeval Crown

and its attendant councillors, and it is not surprising
that Hamilton was charged with cherishing monarchical sentiments and that he thought it wise to remove
himself for a time from the company of men whom
his opinions must have shocked. His powerful ad-
vocacy of the Constitution as it eventually emerged
showed that its provisions were not too remote from
his views, and John Buchan imagined a very plausible
might-have-been in his tale of an American delegation
purposefully visiting the Young Pretender, Prince
Charles Edward, only to find him a besotted drunkard.
The members of the Convention wanted a Constitution on the English pattern because they were English,
and wanted a republic partly because they had dis-
owned their King and partly because it had become
the fashion to be republican. It was then that they
remembered, subconsciously maybe, that the English
monarchy was originally elective, that, as the Act of
Settlement showed, it had never really lost its original
quality, and that it therefore could be made compatible with republican institutions. In theory a monarchy and a republic represent political extremes. In
practice the American President is very nearly the
Tudor monarch with certain eighteenth century re-
finements, functioning, like everything else in the
American political system, under a time-limit.

Other considerations also operated. When the Declaration of Independence was issued the American
Colonies all depended, directly or indirectly, upon the
Crown. They owed their legal status to charters
issued by the King, in the first instance to trading

companies that had subsequently surrendered their rights again to the Crown, later on either to individual or associated proprietors, some of whom had also surrendered their rights, or without any intermediate agency, to settlements that desired to combine and constitute a colony. Government by charter belongs to a very early phase of English constitutional history. Just because the King was elected he had to give certain undertakings in order to secure election. These undertakings originally took the form of charters. William the Conqueror, for example, issued a charter after Hastings in which he declared that he would abide by the laws of King Edward. As a matter of fact, Edward the Confessor had not issued a set of laws at all. Earlier Kings had done so, but their laws were not new enactments but statements of existing customs, often made more definite and sometimes amplified, which the King undertook to observe. These charters culminated in Magna Carta. Subsequent charters repeated its provisions with occasional modifications, and in 1297, eighty-two years after the great charter was issued, the document known as the *Confirmatio Cartarum*, which is really a statute though it takes the form of a charter, incorporated its provisions in the formal law of the land. English constitutional history in the earlier period consists largely of the process of transition from government by charter to government by statute.

There is no parallel transition in American history. When the charter issued by King James I to the London Company authorised the colonisation of Virginia, it provided that the government of the Colony should be conducted from the Company's house in London. This arrangement inevitably broke down and the Virginia Charter had been resumed by the Crown when, in 1629, a charter was issued to the Massachusetts Bay Company as a consequence of the settlement of the Pilgrim Fathers on territory well to the north of the London Company's frontiers. As a majority of the shares in the new Company were held by settlers, this second charter transferred the seat of the government of the Colony from London to colonial soil; and the new policy was further developed later in the century when the grants to proprietors instructed them to obtain the consent of the local freemen to their legislation. Thus, by steps that followed quite naturally from the fact that it took several weeks to cross the Atlantic, the English Parliament was excluded from schemes of colonial development, nor did Parliament take any exception to this exclusion. Representing as it did the English people, it was concerned, and as the seventeenth century wore on became more passionately and vitally concerned, with what the King did at home but was not interested in the King's relations with Englishmen overseas. When Jefferson drafted the Declaration of Independence he formulated it in terms of a series of charges brought against King George III. Such a presentation of the colonists' grievances was not merely tactically expedient but historically sound. Their relations were with the King in person, or possibly with the King in Council, but never with the King in Parliament. On

the contrary, their whole case was that Parliament
had been replaced in the charters to which they owed
their existence by their own local assemblies.

In Jefferson's day the social contract theory dominated political thought. It was already dominant at
the time of the English Revolution, and both King
James II and King George III were accused, the one
in so many words and the other by implication, of
breaking the contracts that they had made with their
people. But the social contract did not mean the same
thing to Englishmen of 1688 and to Americans of
1776. The English contract, though no doubt it implied an ultimate reference to Magna Carta, consisted
in the main of those conventions in the English sense
of the term which, in the course of time, had come to
govern the relations of the Crown with the people's
representatives in Parliament, more particularly in
matters of taxation, but which had not been formulated in precise terms until Coke inspired the Long
Parliament to draw up the Petition of Right. To the
American colonists, on the other hand, the social contract was defined from the first in the charters creating the colonies. In those charters the King had said
that the freemen of the colony were to be consulted
about the laws of the colony, and indeed, colonial
history for the century preceding the Declaration of
Independence is made up very largely of quarrels between the colonial assemblies and the Royal governors, the assemblies passing legislation that the
governors vetoed, or declining to proceed with Bills
that the governors laid before them. The contract

that the King broke in England in the seventeenth century was, as it were, a gentleman's agreement; the contract that he broke in America in the eighteenth was a legal undertaking.

It is among the anomalies of constitutional history that America has and keeps a written Constitution, whereas the English Constitution is not merely unwritten but is so sensitive to the winds of circumstance that it is probably incapable of being committed to writing. The reason for this remarkable difference of attitude towards first principles of government lies in the historical facts just noted. In early English history no charter before Magna Carta was comprehensive enough to be regarded as a constitution. Moreover, a charter was binding only upon the King who issued it, and even upon him only during his good pleasure. Magna Carta itself was only a few months old when the Pope absolved the King from his solemn pledge to observe its provisions. But the charters of the American colonies, just because they were intended to operate in regions far beyond the King's immediate control, were sacred documents from the first.

IN England the Prime Minister is to-day and, with occasional intervals, has been since Walpole's time, the pivot on which the whole constitutional machinery turns. In the United States there is no Prime Minister. The reason is that the Prime Minister is a parliamentary figure, and Parliament was, as it were,

doubly excluded from any place in American constitutional development during the Colonial period. It
was excluded in the first place by the fact that the
colonial charters emanated from the King and that
Parliament had nothing to do with them, and in the
second place by the fact that the responsiveness of the
American Colonies to changes in political circumstances in England ceased when the migration of the
members of the land-owning classes from England
came to an end towards the close of the seventeenth
century. The colonists knew that the King was not
absolute, but they did not know that Parliament was
sovereign.

The British Constitution in the form with which we
are now familiar developed in the century that separates
the English Revolution from the premiership of the
younger Pitt. The immediate cause of the Revolution
was the claim of James II that he was above the law.
William III was definitely subject to the law, though
he was given a veto, which he exercised, over new
legislation. But on the executive side the Revolution
left the position of the Crown substantially unchanged, though developments in Charles II's reign
had already indicated that the King's councillors
would not be tolerated by Parliament unless they
possessed its confidence and that they could prevail
over the King's will when they held it. If in William
III's reign the growth of the party system enhanced
the authority of the leading politicians, the fact did
not appear of great importance at a time when the
main issues were international. William's title to be

both his own foreign minister and his own commander-in-chief was not challenged. The situation,
however, was materially altered by the accession of a
female sovereign. The command of the armies necessarily passed to the one of her subjects who was a soldier
of genius, and while the Queen continued to preside
over the meetings of her councillors held in her cabinet, the wife of her commander-in-chief possessed her
private ear and swayed her will so far and for so long
as to justify Pope's gibe that the Queen sometimes
took council and sometimes tea. The subsequent accession of a sovereign who did not understand England
and could not speak English completed the transfer of authority, whose gradual passage from the
Crown to the party leaders is eminently characteristic
of the English way of doing things.

Authority, which the Crown was no longer in a
condition to exercise, naturally passed to the great
territorial magnates who, in the England of the early
eighteenth century, were the only persons capable of
taking it over. Their positions made them members
of the House of Lords and they were brought into
still more compact relationship with one another in
that they were all members of the same party, the
Whigs, their Tory opponents[3] being of doubtful
loyalty to the dynasty. Since the House of Commons
had in Charles II's reign successfully asserted its exclusive control over supply, it was necessary for the
great Whig Lords to have a manager in the House

---

[3] Their leader Bolingbroke almost succeeded in achieving a
restoration of the Stuarts.

of Commons. That the manager should have gathered all the threads of policy into his own hands so that he was felt to deserve the title of Prime or First Minister, given him in opprobrium by constitutional purists, was due to the peculiar genius of Sir Robert Walpole. Even the elder Pitt did not occupy quite the same position but had to share leadership in the cabinet with the Duke of Newcastle; and when King George III, born and educated, as he said, in England, and glorying in the name of Britain, came to the throne, he availed himself of the old Whig expedient of appointing a manager who would guarantee the acquiescence of the House of Commons in his attempt to recover for the Crown the position it had enjoyed in William III's time. With the language of the Declaration of Independence in their minds Americans naturally associate the name of King George III with the idea of personal rule. Such notions falsify English history—and possibly American history too; for had George III in fact aimed at the establishment of a despotism, he would have looked for a rival to the power of Parliament and might well have found it in Benjamin Franklin's proposal, put forward only a few years before his accession, of a body representative of all the thirteen colonies. With Parliaments on both sides of the Atlantic, the King could have asserted his supreme authority by playing off one against the other. In that case, as his system must have collapsed when his mind gave way, the inevitable separation from the mother country might have taken place without bloodshed. That possibility, however,

F

is another of history's might-have-beens. Actually King George III sought to recover for the Crown not the powers that it had enjoyed before 1640 but those formally conferred upon it in 1689.

Political conditions being what they were, the King's plans called for a party of King's friends in the House of Commons, attached to the Crown because they owed their positions to its favour, and for a party-leader whose policy would give effect to the King's pleasure. After some search the Crown found the man it wanted in Lord North. The American war is important in English constitutional history because it eventually forced Lord North to resign. Casting desperately about for some means of keeping the Whigs, and particularly their hated leader, Fox, out of office, the King charged the younger Pitt to form a ministry and found that he had provided himself not with an agent but with a master. Pitt was the King's nominee and used his position with his sovereign to beat down the hostile majority in the House of Commons. No doubt he could have had a dissolution when he took office; no doubt, too, the Royal influence was strong enough in the counties as well as in the boroughs to have given him a majority. But under those circumstances he would have come back as much the King's manager as Lord North had been. Pitt waited until the majority against him in the House had vanished; then, when he no longer required it, he asked for and obtained a dissolution. Seeking for ground on which he could stand in virtue of his own strength and without dependence on the King's sup-

port, he found it in the device, of which he is the
author, of ministerial appeal to the country. There is
precedent for everything in England, and right at the
end of his reign William III had dissolved Parliament
in an appeal to the country against a Tory ministry.
Pitt turned the Royal weapon against the Crown, and
it was fortunate for the smooth passage of England
to democratic forms of government that the King's
mind gave way when it did and so prevented a fierce
struggle between the King and his politically too-
powerful subject.

Under the arrangements that prevail in Britain to-
day, party government is as much the rule as it was
in the eighteenth century, but the leadership of parties
has passed to those whom parliamentary and public
opinion combine in thinking best suited for the office;
and in a period of emergency this opinion, clearly expressed, is capable of transferring leadership to a man
who, while retaining his party affiliations, stands actually above party and is thus competent to head a coalition ministry. Such in roughest outline is the position
of the Prime Minister, whose office did not establish
its claim to a formal constitutional existence until as
late as 1905, when Mr. Balfour, at the time of his own
resignation, advised the Crown to give the Prime Minister precedence immediately after the Archbishop of
York.

Circumstances trivial in themselves but of weighty
cumulative effect prevented parallel developments in
the American Colonies. There was only one Parliament in England, but each of the thirteen Colonies

had its separate legislature. There was but one King in England, and he retained his position, short of revolution, for as long as he lived. There were thirteen colonial governors and all of them held office for comparatively short terms. Above all, the King had nobody to fall back upon when his Parliament opposed him, but the governors in their conflicts with the colonial assemblies could fall back upon the powerful support of the King. These difficulties might have been overcome had parliamentary development in the Colonies been such as to permit the conception of parliamentary sovereignty to take root. But on the other side of the Atlantic different circumstances caused different traditions to prevail. The House of Representatives does not possess, and short of a revolution could not acquire, powers smiliar to those exercised by the House of Commons. The greatest of all the differences between British and American constitutional practices lies in the widely different measures of authority enjoyed by the Houses composed of the representatives of the people.

III

Parliament and Congress

THE Saxon Kings of England showed their regard for the maxim that government is by the consent of the governed by surrounding themselves with a body of councillors, the wise men or Witan, drawn from the leading personages in their realm. Consultation of the common people was out of the question at so early a stage of political development. It was on the legal side that the common people first participated in the business of government. The average Englishman is quite right in regarding trial by jury as among his fundamental rights. The origins of the jury are uncertain. Probably it goes back to Charlemagne; certainly it had been established in England for centuries before Henry II regularised and amplified the country's judicial system. Respect for the law, which in the first instance meant no more than insistence upon custom, is among the oldest of English traditions, and the Royal officer to whom was entrusted the local maintenance of the King's peace based on law was the shire reeve, or sheriff, who presided over the County Court. The original jurymen were witnesses before him, and witnesses not as to facts but as to character.

They could state of their personal knowledge whether the person accused was the sort of man who would commit a crime. Originally, too, they were witnesses as to custom, which was in fact law, and to this extent they were also judges. The final decision rested with the sheriff, but what was to happen if the jury, who knew both the accused and the law, were dissatisfied with the decision and held that the King's peace had not been properly safeguarded?

To this problem, jurymen gave the very English answer that they would go and talk to the King about it, and as the King spoke Norman French the talk became a parley and the arrangements for it to take place, a parliament. To this day members of the Church of England pray for the High Court of Parliament when it is in session. As far as its own proceedings are concerned, the House of Commons has insisted that it is a court and on occasion the Speaker has issued warrants. As a court the House of Lords has reserved the right to try its own members by a procedure that has been modified only in the last few years. The arrangements whereby certain judges are created life Peers, and hear appeals to the Crown from its courts in Great Britain—appeals that since the abolition of the Court of Star Chamber could not go through any channel other than the House of Lords —are of Victorian origin but are a revival of latent facilities; and the appeals are heard before what is formally a sitting of the House of Lords with the Lord Chancellor presiding.

But the most important of the legal rights of Parliament are connected with impeachment. In impeachment cases the House of Commons conducts the prosecution and the House of Lords tries the case. It may well be that this arrangement, which like so much else in English constitutional history is a matter of convention, was the result of a bargain giving the decisive word in matters of law to the House of Lords and the decisive word in matters of taxation to the House of Commons. In Britain impeachment is now obsolete. The responsibility of ministers to the House of Commons enables a minister to be turned out of office before his conduct has been sufficiently grave to warrant impeachment. The last famous case was the impeachment of Warren Hastings, late in the eighteenth century, and the last recorded case the impeachment of Dundas, early in the nineteenth. Both these cases ended in acquittals.

In the United States the conditions that permit impeachment to become obsolete have not operated. Under the American Constitution with its separation of powers there is no direct and continuous responsibility (in the sense of Parliamentary government) of the executive to Congress. Executive power is centred in the President, and the only way of getting rid of a President during his term of office is to impeach him. One President has actually been impeached— Andrew Johnson, who, as Vice-President, succeeded to the Presidency after Lincoln's assassination and was quickly involved in a violent quarrel with Congress over the policy to be adopted towards the Confederate States. He was acquitted by one vote. Motions for the impeachment of later Presidents, Mr. Hoover being the last on the list, were brought forward from time to time, but nothing more was heard of them. Judges stand in a somewhat similar position. Both the British and the American Constitutions lay the utmost emphasis on the independence of the judiciary, and in England drastic steps have been taken to maintain the position of the judges against the Crown. But a British judge can be removed by means of an address from both Houses of Parliament. In America the separation of powers again forbids a parallel procedure, and an American federal judge can be touched only by impeachment. There is a fairly long list of cases and members of the Supreme Court figure in it.

THE legal beginnings of Parliament are of importance because of their powerful influence upon parliamentary procedure. The men who came up from the country to talk to the King about an alleged act of injustice had a grievance and petitioned the King to redress that grievance, and in this procedure lies the origin of the immensely significant political principle upon which the whole body of English statute law is founded: that redress of grievances must precede supply. Supply had not been thought of when the first rudimentary parliaments submitted their petitions to the Crown. Supply was a consequence of the substitution of a money for a barter economy. There was a period when government meant on the part of the governed an obligation to perform services and on the part of the governors a guarantee of protection in return for them; and this was the system under which the early Norman Kings organised their conquered realm. But before the twelfth century was out the possibility of commuting services for money had to be considered, the more so because the Kings were interested in making war in France and the obligation of vassals to serve their sovereign outside the borders of the realm could be disputed. Clearly the most convenient arrangement was that the King should levy troops for his foreign wars. But these troops needed to be paid, and though it was always intended that the King should live of his own, on the proceeds of the export duty on wool and a source of revenue still called the customs, the import duty on wine regularly granted to him at the beginning of his reign, foreign wars always led to requests for additional funds. They were met by rudimentary taxes on property, and here was a matter that clearly touched every owner of property and on which he was entitled to express his opinions. It is not an accident that until the nineteenth century the right to vote in England was intimately associated with the possession of property. As finally stabilised in the reign of Henry VI, the vote outside the boroughs was conferred on the possessors of freeholds of the value of forty shillings, and this remained the qualification until nearly four centuries later, when leaseholders were enfranchised by the Reform Bill of 1832.

When men began to come up to the capital to talk

to the King not only about injustices committed by
his officials but about finance for his oversea wars,
Parliament was beginning to take shape. What is
called the Model Parliament, which included, in addi-
tion to the magnates, two knights from each shire and
two burgesses from each borough, was summoned by
Edward I in 1295, and it was in reference to his own
financial needs that the King enunciated the old principle of Roman law that what touched all should be
approved by all. Legislation was not at this time regarded as touching all. The most important statutes
of Edward I's reign were not laid before Parliament.
Legislation was the King's business, to be transacted
in co-operation with his council and particularly, as
the matter of legislation became more complex, with
his judges. Much later, in Tudor times, when the
right of the two Houses to pass statutes was explicitly
recognised, Bills laid before Parliament were drafted
by the judges, and appear to have been finally revised
by the judges before they received the Royal assent,
which was not then a matter of form. To this day the
law officers of the Crown receive separate and individual summonses (which they ignore) to the meeting of Parliament, and when the King delivers the
speech from the Throne a group of judges sit on a
bench immediately facing it.

The two Houses of Parliament have met separately
since at least as early as the middle of the fourteenth
century, but the Parliament that the King addresses in
person is only one body. In England the old tradition
is faithfully maintained. Parliaments are summoned

by the King, they meet in a Royal Palace, and they meet in a room containing a Throne. From this Throne the mediaeval King informed Parliament of his needs and then withdrew, as he withdraws now. The great Lords stayed behind to discuss the matter. The Commons felt uncomfortable in the presence of such distinguished persons. Moreover, there was no room to sit down. So they sought to withdraw to a place of their own where they could talk things over, and the monks of the Abbey of Westminster obliged by the loan of their Chapter House, in which the House of Commons continued to meet until 1547. The size of the Chapter House is evidence that the early House of Commons was not a large body. The boroughs in particular grumbled at the expense of having to send to London representatives whom they had to pay, and one borough, Torrington in Devon, has won a text-book immortality by securing perpetual release from the obligation of sending two of its burgesses to Parliament. Often, too, the Royal writ was ignored; in many fourteenth and early fifteenth century Parliaments borough representatives did not number more than half a dozen. It is probable that the early Parliaments broke up into sections representing various interests or, in mediaeval language, estates. The merchants probably taxed themselves separately. The clergy certainly did so, authorising in convocation taxes that were later approved by Parliament under an arrangement that continued until after the Restoration, when it was brought to a close by a verbal agreement between the Lord Chancellor and the Archbishop of Canterbury.

It followed from the whole purpose of Parliament that both counties and boroughs required to be represented by local men, since only a local man could say what the people in his part of the country were likely to think about the King's demands. But it also followed that, at any rate in the more distant parts of the realm, a desire would manifest itself to save money by choosing a representative who did not live too far from London, and the obligation to elect a local resident was therefore made statutory in 1413. This Statute was not formally repealed until 1774, but the obligation had long ceased to be observed and the plea that it had fallen into desuetude was successfully raised against an attempt to enforce it—the only plea of its kind in the whole history of English law. In the United States the local condition is still operative. The United States is a federation and it is accordingly felt proper that in both Houses of Congress the States should be represented by persons resident within their borders. The Constitution goes no further than this. But convention in the English sense of the term has also laid down that a member of the House of Representatives must be a resident in the congressional district for which he is returned.

This arrangement is largely responsible for the weakness of the House of Representatives as compared with the House of Commons. Over large areas of the United States representation remains permanently under the control of the same party. The

North-East is overwhelmingly Republican; the South is proverbially solid for the Democrats. It follows that an American who cherishes political ambitions can never become a member of either House of Congress if holding Republican opinions he lives, for example, in Alabama, or holding Democratic opinions he lives, for example, in Maine; and this is how it comes about that men who have had no congressional experience can become figures in national politics and even as presidential candidates.

To-day both Congress and Parliament meet annually, the former under the provisions of the Constitution, the latter under an arrangement that developed almost accidentally at the beginning of William III's reign. Earlier Kings had received their traditional revenues—the customs—for life, and accordingly summoned a Parliament only when they wanted more money. But William III's first Parliament was suspicious of a Crown handsomely endowed and therefore no longer under control. In spite of the King's protests it conferred the customary revenues for one year only. The arrangement has been maintained ever since, and as neither the military forces nor the civil servants of the Crown can be paid without a grant of revenue, Parliament necessarily meets every year to vote supply.

In England supply was the only matter to which Parliament necessarily attended from the very beginning, though in fact, like Congress, it has become predominantly an instrument of legislation. But the legislative rights of Congress are explicitly conferred upon it by the Constitution, which makes it impossible for legislation to originate from any other source, whereas in England Parliament's legislative powers are the results of gradual but sustained encroachments. In its early days Parliament could petition the Crown to redress a grievance and if the grievance were general it could best be redressed by the passage of a law. As a means of compelling the Crown to give ear to its petitions Parliament made it clear that until its grievances had been redressed it would not vote the supply desired by the Crown. It often happened, however, that while the Crown got its supply on the strength of an undertaking to redress submitted grievances, Parliament was subsequently dissatisfied with the way in which the undertaking was carried out, if, indeed, its execution was not postponed indefinitely. Parliament therefore hit on the device of incorporating in its petitions the remedy that it desired, and, by a natural course of development, what started as a petition became a Bill with the petitionary part confined to the preamble or omitted altogether. Parliamentary Bills continue to bear traces of their origin in the formula of enactment with which they open, but the words "Be it enacted by the King's Most Excellent Majesty," originally a prayer, have become in effect a command.

All this tradition survived in the American Colonies to the extent of making it inevitable that Congress should be the instrument of legislation, but with the disappearance of the Crown the formula of enactment of Congressional Bills was necessarily changed and the long historical struggle that has placed power in the hands of the representatives of the people has left no trace on the formal language of an Act of Congress. Though traditions that have died out in England frequently remain active in the United States, the War of Independence effectively scrapped the most ancient tradition of all: in England the Royal assent, by which a Bill becomes law, is still given in Norman French: "Le Roi le veult," though the House of Commons has recorded its proceedings in English since the year 1414. In America the arrangements for the Presidential assent derive from nothing more ancient than the English Revolution. The events of 1688 left the Crown with a power of veto, which was occasionally exercised for twenty years and then lapsed. In the United States the Presidential veto is still active and is regularly used, though it may be overcome by a two-thirds vote in both Houses.

INSTITUTIONS do not work of themselves. They are what they are made by the men who function under them. A striking feature common to both Parliament and Congress is the important part played by lawyers in their proceedings. This strong representation of the law in politics is not due wholly to the fact that the English are a law-abiding people and that the Americans carried on their tradition—so emphatically, indeed, that a minor but deliberate act of lawlessness such as the Boston Tea Party is rightly taken to be an outstanding historical event. The large number of lawyers in the early English Parliaments, and particularly in the Lower House, was due to the fact that they constituted the only class of men for whom prolonged absences in London did not occasion a serious disturbance of the normal course of their lives. They had business in the King's Courts at Westminster and they were prepared to kill two birds with one stone, the more so because their expenses were paid by their constituents if they could go to the capital as members of Parliament. Indeed, in Edward III's reign the knights of the shire who went up to Parliament as a matter of public duty were so disturbed at the growing number in their ranks of lawyers who found it convenient to combine politics with their profession that they caused a statute to be passed making lawyers who practised in the King's courts ineligible for election on the ground that they were using their representative position to attract clients.

The statute did not keep lawyers out of the House and the problem was eventually solved in a different way. The House as a whole took up individual petitions that its lawyer members laid before it, being stirred to do so partly by the fact that Parliament itself was a High Court and partly by the fact that its business was to get grievances redressed. This was the origin of private bill legislation. Private bills in Britain now-a-days are normally promoted by municipalities, railway companies, and other large organisations, but individual cases normally are not taken up. Until the first Divorce Act was passed in

1857, however, a private bill was the only means by which a marriage could be legally dissolved, and at a somewhat earlier period it was the only means by which a landowner could enclose waste or common land. Individual private bills have a much longer history in America, where they are the orthodox means of bestowing pensions upon allegedly deserving individuals and where they were passed literally by the thousands until late in the nineteenth century, when President Cleveland had the courage to veto them *en bloc*.

Long after a seat in Parliament had ceased to further a practising lawyer's professional ambition, the law continued to supply more than its due proportion of members because parliamentary life was not incompatible with a practice at the Bar. Until fairly recently the sittings of the House began only shortly before the Courts rose for the day; it is the heavy committee work in the mornings that nowadays makes it difficult for a lawyer to find time both for his professional work and his Parliamentary duties, and that, with the increasing length of sessions, is turning politics into a separate profession. There were, however, other and more cogent reasons for the presence of a large contingent of lawyers in the mediaeval House of Commons. With the clergy ineligible, they were the only class in the community who were completely literate and at their ease when handling documents. Not until after the redistribution of land, which was one of the consequences of the Reformation, did there arise in England a class of gentlemen

G

of independent means who were marked out by their
position to represent their communities and by their
inclinations to undertake public duties. The course of
land settlement in America has obstructed the emergence of such a class, and even more than in England
the average American business man is too completely
occupied with his own affairs to have time to attend
to politics. The causes that brought about a preponderance of lawyers in the early English Parliaments
are thus still operative in the United States; more than
half the members of the modern House of Representatives are lawyers by profession.

It contributes greatly to the smooth working of
American institutions that this should be the case, because the relationship between the legislature and the
courts is much closer in America, both in national
politics and in the States, than it is in England. In
England there is never any doubt that an Act of Parliament is the law of the land, but in America a Bill
duly passed by the legislature still faces the possibility
of being questioned as to whether it is in accordance
with the Constitution either of a State or of the
United States. It is all to the good that this question
should be discussed by keen legal minds while the Bill
is still in draft and that the Courts, which eventually
will have to pronounce upon it, should be left in no
doubt whether in the opinion of its promoters the
Bill lies comfortably within the framework of the
Constitution or is an attempt to give new elasticity to
the provisions of the latter.

Whether the existence or non-existence of a large

and public-spirited leisured class is politically advantageous may well be a matter of dispute. In England the leisured class dominated English politics from the Long Parliament until the close of Queen Victoria's reign. In the easy-going eighteenth century it took full advantage of its opportunities, and grave abuses crept in under the cover of maintaining the Revolution settlement. The vision of even high-minded men is limited by their circumstances, and the leisured class has left behind it in England a memory of legislation in the interests of members of their own body that nowadays arouses some bitterness and threatens reprisals in kind from those who were so long the under-privileged. In the United States the Southern States, and particularly Virginia, were prepared to supply Congress with senators and representatives drawn from the body of large-scale landowners, and did supply them during the first generation of the Constitution's history. It is worth noting that in this period the House of Representatives was a stronger element in the Constitution than it has ever been since, and that with the transfer of political power to the new frontier states of the Middle West and to the rapidly growing commercial and industrial states of the North-East pre-eminence passed to the Senate in which the old-fashioned type of American gentleman continued to sit up to the time of the Civil War. But though there was nothing in American constitutional history to correspond to the long predominance of county families in the House of Commons, abuses have slipped into American politics under cover of the Constitution at least as easily as they crept into English politics under the cover of the Revolution Settlement. It is true in both countries that the price of political honesty no less than of political liberty is eternal vigilance and that temptations to the private acquisition of public funds will not be resisted by any representative body unless it feels itself responsible to a vigorous and well-informed public opinion.

PARTIES

THROUGHOUT the English-speaking world, politics are party politics. But neither in England nor in the United States is it immediately clear why parties should have acquired their present hold on the political system. In England the origins of party can be traced back to Tudor times, and the first great split in English politics occurred over religion. Religion, however, is one of the subjects on which men cannot easily agree to differ because they cannot admit that there are two sides to the question. The truth that they hold is the whole truth; those who disagree with them are damned eternally, and discussion is futile. Two circumstances, however, made it possible for parties to develop in England around the religious core. The first was the overwhelming strength in Tudor times of the position of the Crown. Nowadays it is Parliament's business to take decisions but in Tudor times decision lay with the Sovereign to whom Parliament could at best make humble representations. Secondly, the House of Commons, which was steadily gaining in strength throughout the Tudor period, has always felt that its main business was the redress of grievances, and in the later sixteenth century it was clear that both Catholics and Puritans had a grievance. So long, however, as political controversies continued to be conducted on religious lines, party development could not have proceeded far without threatening to break up Parliament altogether. A very different situation was created when the religious issue in the form in which it was presented to the House of Commons became a part of the more general issue of the relations of Parliament with the Crown. In its earlier dealings with the Stuart Kings the House of Commons was almost, if not quite, unanimous. The cleavage came when Parliament made claims on the Crown that, though they might be presented as the reassertion of ancient privileges, involved a real transfer of power. Such a situation arose with the preparation of the Grand Remonstrance in 1641. It was finally carried by a majority of eleven, and parties as England has since known them really originated with that historic division.

The position that it created was full of peril, and the peril was not averted. The Civil War turned the Long Parliament into the Rump, and it was only after years of painful experience that opinion throughout the country determined on the maintenance of the monarchy. Then the members whom the Rump had so long excluded returned to their seats; the Long Parliament became its true self again and made the Restoration certain before it declared itself dissolved. After the Restoration the development of parties was again overshadowed, faintly in the reign of

Charles II, sharply in the reign of his successor, by
the old issue of parliamentary versus regal powers.

Even nowadays when English history is no longer
viewed through orthodox Liberal spectacles it is
something of a paradox to suggest that Charles II was
less of a constitutional King than his brother and successor. But when Charles accepted a pension from
Louis XIV he undermined the power of the purse
upon which Parliamentary influence over the Crown
was based, whereas James II sought only to assert the
Royal prerogative in a region in which it had never
been clearly defined. The laws in regard to which he
claimed both a suspending and a dispensing power
were religious laws, and his prerogative flowed from
his position as Supreme Governor of the Church of
England. This title had been bestowed on Queen
Elizabeth rather more than a century before in substitution for that of Supreme Head assumed by Henry
VIII. A certain discretion in the application of laws
is permitted to every government—at the present day
it is accorded to the Home Secretary when he exercises the prerogative of mercy on the Crown's behalf
—and, at any rate as regards the dispensing power,
James II had something of a constitutional case. But
whereas Charles II's action was personal and was in
any case not likely to survive the next crisis in European affairs, James II was seeking to assert new powers
not for himself but for the Crown, and to assert them
to the confusion of the Reformation settlement on
whose maintenance in principle the internal peace of
the realm depended. In the last resort Charles II un-

derstood his people and knew how far he could go, whereas James II with his strong inheritance of Stuart doctrinarism did not; and so Charles was never in real danger of going on his travels again, whereas his brother was driven into exile.

In the last thirty years of the formative seventeenth century, while the religious issue was still brewing, the constitutional situation gradually cleared up. It became clear first that the King could not administer public affairs with their growing complexity without the daily assistance of a body of councillors, and, secondly, that the administrative work of those councillors could not be effective unless they possessed the confidence of Parliament. One further step remained to be taken, a step that appears easy in retrospect but that must have seemed extraordinarily bold to those who actually took it. Perhaps, indeed, it would never have been taken but for the combination after the death of William III of the emergency of a great war and the presence of a woman on the Throne.

The situation presented itself in somewhat different but happily converging terms to the parties principally concerned, the Crown and the House of Commons. To the Crown it became apparent that the Council would prove a broken reed unless it were unanimous. Failing unanimity, the grave matters under discussion rendered violent disagreement certain, and if her councillors tendered contradictory advice what was the Queen to do? From the point of view of the House of Commons it became clear that the responsibility to itself that it desired to assert could only be imposed

on the councillors as a body. It might well be that one
of its members drew upon himself the special censure
of the House, but even if, as a consequence of that
censure, he was forced to resign, the general policy
that had resulted in his censured action was likely
enough to be continued by his colleagues who had
not resigned because they had not been attacked, and
then what was the House of Commons to do? The
only possible answer that either the Queen or the
House could give was that there must be a body of
ministers so united that if one were attacked and fell
the others necessarily fell with him, and the only
sentiment that could create the political tie thus felt to
be essential was the sentiment of party. It is no doubt
true that differences in religious outlook, differences
in opinion as to the powers of the Crown, and differences of economic views between townsmen and
countrymen, all helped to create a definite line of
party cleavage. But what made the dominance of
party feeling politically necessary was that the relations between the Crown and Parliament had now
reached such a stage that only a united ministry responsible, though in slightly different senses of the
term, to both, could enable them to function smoothly.
The device was characteristically English in that it
evaded the fundamental question which, if definitely
raised, would have divided Englishmen into monarch-
ists and republicans and produced another Civil War.
But evasive though it was, the arrangement worked
and still works. To this day the Crown nominally

appoints ministers [1] and the real confidence of the House of Commons keeps them in office.

The reign of Anne is generally and rightly regarded as marking the triumph of party in English political affairs. Two qualifications need, however, to be borne in mind. First, parties had been felt to be not quite respectable. They received opprobrious nicknames— Whigs from lawless Scottish Covenanters, and Tories from, if anything, slightly more lawless Irish Catholics —and the names stuck. Secondly, it is true that Queen Anne fought the great war with a Whig ministry but a Tory ministry made the peace that ended it. As her reign went on, the members of the Council became more and more definitely of the same party complexion. But her death created a crisis and at the height of that crisis two great Whig Lords, Somerset and Argyll, dashed to London, broke in on the Council, which was not itself of one mind on the dynastic issue, and by their intervention made it certain that the heralds should proclaim King George and not King James. What the two Whig Lords had in fact done, as they may themselves perhaps have realised, was to turn out the Tory ministry without the formality of a Parliamentary vote.

The accession of George I made a Whig Government certain because the loyalty of the Tories could

---

[1] The normal procedure is that, on tendering his resignation, a retiring Prime Minister advises the Sovereign for whom he should send. The party leader sent for is invited to form an administration. If the invitation is accepted the new Prime Minister submits a list of appointments to his Cabinet for formal approval.

not be trusted,[2] and the Whigs continued in office
for as long as this situation prevailed, that is to say
until the accession of George III in 1760, by which
time Jacobitism had become no more than a romantic
memory. The Whigs fell from power as soon as the
circumstances that had put them into power ceased to
operate, and by the swing of the political pendulum
their half-century of power was followed by an even
longer period of almost unbroken opposition. It
speaks volumes for the hold that party had obtained
over political thought in England that party lines
remained firmly drawn when first one party and then
the other was out of office for fifty years at a time;
and it is because party was established in the English
constitutional fabric that, when the old party divisions
became obsolete after the growth of industrialism and
the rise of the middle class, party organisations, though
with new names, could still dominate the political
scene and determine the composition of Parliaments.

It is significant of the extent to which the American
Colonies had become intellectually divorced from the
Mother country and had developed their own methods of thought, that the whole of this remarkable
development of party in eighteenth century Britain
was ignored by the Philadelphia Convention. Plan-
ning for the United States as a whole, the Convention
had to transcend party, and Madison, who appears

[2] See p. 43, *supra*, n.

from the records to have done more than any member
to guide its proceedings, afterwards expressed himself
on the matter with a warmth of language unusual with
him. "The history of almost all the great councils
and consultations held among mankind for reconciling
their discordant opinions . . . may be classed among
the most dark and degraded pictures which display
the infirmities and depravities of the human character." Now and again an exception is found, and when
it occurs "the convention must have enjoyed in a very
singular degree an exemption from the pestilential influence of party animosity—the disease most incident
to deliberative bodies, and most apt to contaminate
their proceedings". (*Federalist*, No. 37).

In fact, the line of division in the Philadelphia Convention was between large and small States, with the
slavery issue looming in the background, so that the
already traditional differences between British Whigs
and Tories were not likely to affect its proceedings.
But Madison went much further. He assumed that
party feeling would play no part in the political life
of the United States as a whole. Mankind are disposed, he frigidly observed "to fall into mutual ani-
mosities" so that "where no substantial occasion
presents itself, the most frivolous and fanciful distinc-
tions have been sufficient to kindle their unfriendly
passions and excite their most violent conflicts". The
English political developments of the past century
having been dismissed in this off-hand fashion, Madison
proceeded in his most professorial style to lay down
the true lines of division between the members of the

same community. "A landed interest, a manufacturing interest, a mercantile interest, a moneyed interest,
with many lesser interests, grow up of necessity in
civilised nations, and divide them into different classes,
actuated by different sentiments and views. The regulation of these various and interfering interests forms
the principal task of modern legislation and involves
the spirit of party and faction in the necessary and
ordinary operations of the Government." (*Federalist*,
No. 10). Similarly Hamilton, with some appreciation
of the part that the leisured classes played in the politics of his time, pointed out that mechanics and artisans
would normally vote for merchants, and small landowners for their richer fellows, so that "from the
natural operation of the different interests and views
of the various classes of the community, whether the
representation of the people be more or less numerous,
it will consist almost entirely of proprietors of land,
of merchants, and of members of the learned professions who will truly represent all those different interests and views". (*Federalist*, No. 35).

In thus translating political divisions into economic
terms, both Madison and Hamilton were well ahead
of their time, but they missed the whole meaning of
party to contemporary minds, with consequences that
have affected, and perhaps dominated, the whole
course of American politics. Madison and Hamilton
both argued that the various interests which would
seek to express themselves in Congress would be essentially local and that the size and comprehensiveness
of the American federation would cause them to

cancel one another out and make it impossible for there to be a majority of interests permanently controlling the minority. On the whole this has proved to be a shrewd analysis. The two great American parties are combinations of interests, and their strength is local, though locality embraces a much wider area than either Madison or Hamilton ever contemplated. Roughly speaking, the States of the Union to-day fall into four main groups: the manufacturing North-Eastern group, which is in the main Republican, the Agricultural South, which is overwhelmingly Democratic, the central farming States, whose support is sought by both parties, and the still mainly agricultural and grazing but rapidly industrialising West, whose rising importance is one of the major political developments of the present century. It is the constant endeavour of both the political parties to extend their influence beyond their respective citadels by forming alliances with either, or preferably both, of the two uncertain groups and so to assure themselves at any rate of the presidency and it may be of majorities in Congress as well. Such tactics demand, and have brought about, a high degree of political organisation, and have yet enabled the English party tradition to develop luxuriantly on the American side of the Atlantic.

The development has been slow. In the first thirty years of the Constitution's history a real line of party cleavage presented itself. There were those who wished to exploit to the utmost the powers assigned to the Federal Government and there were those who were emphatic in the assertion of States rights. The former group took the name of Federalists, the latter, by way of calling attention not merely to the existence but to the quality of their States, called themselves Republicans. This second group, to the confusion of English students, became the spiritual fathers of the modern Democrats. Neither of the original parties had the breath of life in them. The Federalists, rightly foreseeing the power of money in a community that would need capital to develop its magnificent untapped resources, aimed at the establishment of an effective central bank. They did not entirely achieve their object and the severe shock sustained by the American economy as recently as 1933 suggested that new approaches had still to be discovered. But by 1820 the Federalists had won all along the line and their party fell to pieces for lack of new worlds to conquer. A little later, the need of party being felt as a means of organising the electorate, the name Whig was borrowed from English politics but could not bear transplantation to American soil, and it was not until the slavery question became acute that the old Federalist Party re-emerged, this time with the name Republican, the reference being not to the many republics that composed the States but to the one great republic that was over them all.

The fate of the earlier Republican Party was even more pitiful. If the Federalists starved, the original Republicans died of over-feeding. In the first generation of the Constitution's life, ten new States were added to the original thirteen and it was clearly necessary for these young communities to become properly self-conscious before any party insistent upon States rights could become a political force. But the self-consciousness that eventually found political expression was that generated on the frontier. The great expansion of America from the Atlantic to the Pacific produced the typical American man as the nineteenth century knew him, a sturdy individualist, used to grappling with nature and contemptuous of the usages, social no less than political, of the older organised societies back East. These men were the American Democracy, which first asserted its political rights with the election of Andrew Jackson to the presidency in 1828, and it is among the little ironies of history that the name Democrat came particularly to attach itself to those who held that one man had a perfect title to own another provided that his skin was of a different colour.

In England, party has been integrated into the fabric of government. In America, with all powers neatly distributed under the provisions of the Constitution, it could not be, and the result has been an elephantiasis of party that is at once all-pervading and wholly irresponsible. Private Willis's observation in Gilbert and Sullivan's opera "Iolanthe'" that:

> "Every boy and every gal
> That comes into this world alive
> Is either a little Liberal
> Or else a little Conservative"

was ceasing to be true at the time when it was first

uttered. In that gay opera itself Strephon enters
Parliament as a Liberal Unionist and so secures the
vote of both the traditional Parties, and there have
been many new developments since then. But in the
United States, in spite of occasional third parties,
which are generally local in character, such as the
Farmer Labour Movement, it is on the whole fair to
assert—paraphrasing Gilbert's rhyme—that every foreign immigrant's brat grew into a real American man
by becoming a little Democrat or else a little Republican. It is in assimilating the immense foreign immi-
gration that the two great American parties have
principally justified their existence. They have been
schools of citizenship, and not very well-conducted
schools either. The absence of social services until
quite recently in a country that was exceptionally
well able to afford them has given the parties their
chance. To the local organiser, called the precinct
captain, the immigrant looked for a job and for help
if he got into trouble. There is something of the
Friendly Society about both the American Parties.
But it is a Friendly Society partisan in intention and
often unscrupulous in method. What it wants from
its members is votes, and in so far as the members are
willing to give their votes, they are well looked after
in return.

So comprehensive are the organisations and so
elastic the principles of the two traditional parties
that attempts to break down their monopoly of national politics have regularly failed and now appear to
have been abandoned. It is significant that there is no

H

nation-wide Labour Party in the United States. The class consciousness implicit in the name is antipathetic to American thought, and although, as British experience has shown, this limitation can be transcended, a serious practical difficulty is presented by the lack of unity in the American Labour movement. But account must also be taken of another factor of great moment in the practical working of American politics.

The range of opinion included in each of the historical parties is very wide, so that a new idea—and new parties stand for new ideas—though initially more congenial to the traditions of one party, may nevertheless hope to commend itself to progressive elements in the other. Moreover, any new line of policy must reckon with the possibility, constantly present to American minds, that its expression in terms of law may call for constitutional amendment. It is therefore both natural and expedient for the advocates of a new idea to form themselves into a pressure group capable of exerting influence upon both parties and of supporting either of them as circumstances demand. Thus the younger and bolder of the two American Labour federations formed during the 1944 presidential campaign a Political Action Committee, which worked actively for Mr. Roosevelt but which forced the Republican candidate to mitigate his statements by declaring that certain achievements of the New Deal had come to stay. Its effective work has promptly reacted upon the organisation of other minority movements; both the Communist and the Socialist parties now act rather as pressure groups than as political parties.

It follows from the elasticity of the party creeds that personal ties are an important factor in American party life. The not infrequent rule of the "boss," the man able to dominate a local party machine and make it serve his own ends, illustrates their strength. Like Walpole, the "boss" is aware that every man has his price, and American feeling is not necessarily scandalised when it is paid. The way is thus open to corrupt practices such as have often disfigured American politics. But zealous service need not be, and perhaps in most cases is not, the consequence of a bargain best kept dark. It may be the result of enthusiasm for a man of special distinction, and an enthusiasm so warm that it may transcend party feeling. A precinct captain may change sides and take the bulk of his following along with him because he has been bought over or because the local candidate of the opposite party is a man whom he admires.

The same considerations apply in national politics, and the fact that the President is both important and well known enables him to look for support outside the circle of his political supporters. President Roosevelt appointed Republicans, one of them an ex-Secretary of State, to the headship of some service departments. There were Democrats in President Hoover's cabinet and the late Mr. Wendell Willkie was not barred in his bid for nomination as Republican candidate for the Presidency in 1940 by his admission that he had voted for Mr. Roosevelt both in 1932 and 1936.

Of the matters about which he is voting, covering, as they do, federal, state and local affairs all at once, the average party member is at best, unless he is a specialist in such matters, imperfectly informed, and at worst, if he is recently naturalised, not informed at all. He therefore generally votes the ticket, that is to say, the whole list of candidates put forward by his party. It must needs be a fairly long list, especially in presidential years, when the vote is given not directly for the presidential candidate but for members of the College of Electors, and it is sometimes enormous. Indeed, ballots bearing three hundred, and even more than four hundred, names are not uncommon.

The organisers of parties naturally expect to be rewarded for all their trouble and expense, and this expectation has led to the development of the spoils system. The system is an old one and was originally devised more than a century ago in the interests of the new democracy, which felt that the gentlemen back East had managed to secure all the good posts for themselves. Its operation has long prevented the emergence in the United States of a civil service on British lines. It is true that since the passage of the Pendleton Act, in 1883, civil service reform based on the merit system has made much progress in the United States. The various new arrangements now comprehend all the lower and middle ranks of the Civil Service; but they have, on the whole, stopped short of the higher posts, which are too valuable for the parties to give up entirely.[3]

American democracy has been no more successful in its effort to break the power of the party managers by means of direct primaries, that is to say, preliminary elections in which candidates are nominated. Nominations are of great importance over the large areas of the United States that are permanently attached to one party, whose nominees are sure to be returned. What the direct primary does is to choose between rival candidates of the same party, thus performing much the same duty as was discharged under the constitution of the Third French Republic by the second ballots held after instead of before the election. But where the party organisation is really strong, the direct primary is as farcical as the election. The names of the candidates are often settled in a preliminary and unofficial party convention, so that in the primary, as in the election, the voter has nothing more to do than vote the ticket. Nevertheless the primaries do sometimes decide between rival groups and candidates within the party organisation.

The Englishman's comment on parties in the United States is identical with the European's comment on parties in England—that there is no real difference

---

[3] In fact, approximately 90 per cent of all federal employees are now covered by civil service regulations; and promotion from the ranks to the very top is no longer unknown in the United States. Critics, however, have stressed the deficiencies of the system as compared with the British. Even on the lower levels, there are many problems of classification and pay-schedules, of training, efficiency standards and promotion, and others, that still wait solution.

between them. This is true and must needs be true so long as there is general agreement on the structure of the State. In so far as this truth is peculiarly applicable to American parties, it follows from the conditions under·which they operate. In any country in which majority rule prevails a party bidding for office must seek to be all things to all voters, but in no country is the electorate so little homogeneous as in the United States. In practice, therefore, the business of both parties is to teach the American way of life to persons to whom it is not traditional. It is when considered as interpretations of a way of life that the two parties reveal their contrariety. Man is a social animal; he is also a free personality; and practical politics consist largely in adjustments of the balance between communal and individual requirements. Broadly speaking the Republican attitude is individualistic and maintains that, given legal equality of opportunity for himself and certain safeguards against the abuse of freedom by others, the citizen can and should be left to shape his own life and should feel accountable to himself for its success or failure; whereas the Democratic philosophy recognises the responsibility of society for the welfare of its members and, stressing "equality of opportunity" as an economic problem, regards the assurance of a livelihood for all as a social duty. In Britain the same basic distinction holds and accounts for the persistent tendency towards a two party system in spite of the occasional emergence of third parties. Hence in both countries the two parties can unite when the challenge to the national way of

life comes from without, but become acutely conscious of their differences when it arises from within.

In the actual evolution of parties, however, on both
sides of the Atlantic, this parallellism of initial outlook has been subjected to the influence of widely
differing circumstances. In Britain a common way
of life, that had gradually established itself in the
course of centuries, was challenged by the despotic
claims of the Stuart Kings, and the origins of parties
can be traced back to the constitutional struggles of
the seventeenth century. When, a hundred years
after the expulsion of the Stuarts, the progress of the
industrial revolution called for a restatement of the
British way of life in new economic terms, both
the historic parties were so firmly established that they
could successfully claim to handle the new issues and
another century was to elapse before a new party
born of industrialism began to make its voice heard.
In the United States, the War of Independence, which
shaped the future of America even more conspicu-
ously than the Great Rebellion shaped the future of
Britain, was fought against a challenge from without
and therefore forbade, instead of stimulating, the
growth of party feeling. In the debates on the Constitution, which were concerned with internal issues,
opinion began to form along party lines—a development roundly condemned by Madison who saw in it
a threat to national unity. In the event the success of
the new institutions and the rapid westward expansion
of the United States quickly put these original divisions out of date and the American way of life as es-

tablished in the first fifty years after independence was shaped by opportunity and not by party.

Not until the slavery issue forced itself into prominence did party assume the importance in the United States which it had long engaged in Britain, and it is because the Civil War compelled, as no other internal event before or since, a restatement of the essential qualities of the American way of life that both parties continue to this day to invoke its traditions.

President (Lawrence) Lowell of Harvard once observed that the organisations of both the great nineteenth century English parties were shams, the one transparent and the other opaque. Similarly the traditional appeals of both the American parties are shams, as perhaps any traditional appeal must be, in a country that takes a pride in moving with the times and of whose population a considerable, though now diminishing, proportion is of foreign birth. Tradition needs to be doctored before it can be brought into effective relation with contemporary facts. Nevertheless the development of both American parties has been influenced by their respective traditions. The Republicans look back to the "real" America—the America which, more than ever in the generation after the Civil War, moved towards the fulfilment of its manifest destiny. Hence the voting strength of the Republican Party is predominantly rural and Protestant, though the power that dominates it is that of Big Business with its encouragement of the sturdy American individualism that favours competition and dislikes Government interference. By a parallel process the Democrats, traditional upholders of the States against the encroachments of a too-powerful federal authority, have become the champions of the underdog. Their voting strength is therefore to be sought in the cities, and particularly among Catholic and other minority elements. It may be that these lines of cleavage will one day become real. Perhaps indeed, they have become real since 1932—at any rate real enough for the Democratic Party's egalitarian tendencies to scandalise its traditional supporters in the South. But for the present at any rate both parties close their ranks every four years in support of their candidates for the Presidency—the great prize whose capture is their one constant aim. Here tradition counts to an extent rather surprising to an Englishman familiar with the immense floating vote that in his country nowadays decides elections. In the United States membership of parties is still largely hereditary, as in the eighteenth century England,[4] and both organisations strive to keep it so.

But for all the sham elements in their organisation, the American parties are not in themselves shams. They represent one of the basic realities of American life. From its first beginnings colonisation in North America has aimed at the establishment of a society and a way of life more perfect than any existing in the old world, and a readiness to attempt short cuts to the

---

[4] Compare, however, the wicked Victorian story:— "Yes, my father was a Conservative, and my grandfather was a Conservative, so I'm a Conservative." "Why, you might as well say 'my father was a thief and my grandfather was a thief, so I'm a thief." "No, then I should have been a Liberal."

ideal is a feature of the American temperament. But in the United States as elsewhere, ideals come up against hard facts, and the perfectibility of mankind has to be sought amid the hazards of the daily struggle for life. More than that, there have at all times been rival ways of approach to the perfect state. American life has been distinguished by the acceptance of a certain degree of social tension. The Englishman likes things to go smoothly and proverbially refuses to meet trouble half-way. But the American knows that trouble must be met and likes to feel that he is out looking for it. This attitude which might lead, and has once led, to the most bitter antagonism is tempered by the reflection that it takes all sorts to make a world, particularly in a country so large and various as the United States with a population to which so many and such diverse strains have contributed.

This underlying social tension expresses itself in various forms—religiously between Protestant and Catholic, socially between town and country, economically between individual enterprise and planned controls, between protectionists and low tariff advocates, and constitutionally in conflicts between the separated powers. In England a repudiation by Parliament of a policy recommended by the executive Government causes a political crisis; in America it is among the accepted possibilities of the Constitution. In national politics it is by no means unusual for the President to be at variance with one or both Houses of Congress, and in the States a dispute between the governor and his legislature is accepted as evidence of proper constitutional activity on both sides. While the Englishman soon tires of political disputes and wishes that the parties would stop quarrelling and get on with a job, the American looks to controversy to add sparkle and excitement to life. The parties, always in conflict because some sort of an election is always impending, give to politics that zest that is so congenial to American feeling and give it the more effectively because their energies are so often expended on mock heroics. But in the last resort they are based upon something solid and really expressive of the national will. The hold of the Republicans on the public mind is strong enough to stop the Democrats from again running a Catholic for the Presidency,[5] and the appeal of Democratic policies has compelled Republicans to insist that certain New Deal principles have come to stay. No doubt the parties are adroit in trimming their sails to catch the passing breeze; but their manoeuvres illustrate the truth that, for the community as for the individual, life offers a perpetual choice of alternatives: and because Americans like to be constantly reminded of this choice, the parties are strong and will endure.

---

[5] Yet the well-publicised discovery of an illegitimate child did not exclude either the Democrat Cleveland or the Republican Harding.

V

SENATE AND HOUSE OF LORDS

SUCH is the kind of machinery whereby the representatives of the people of Britain and America find their way into their respective legislatures. A further discipline awaits them in the two Houses of which each legislature is composed. The United States Senate is the strongest and the House of Lords the weakest of all upper Houses in the world to-day, and while the structure of the Senate has supplied a working model to other federal states, no country has copied the House of Lords, which was not even the deliberate creation of the English themselves.

In its origins the House of Lords consisted of those subjects of the Crown whose importance caused them to be summoned as individuals. There is some uncertainty as to the period at which the possession of the peerage entitled the holder to a writ of summons. In the earlier stages of Parliamentary history the King appears to have summoned whom he chose. At a somewhat later date a writ issued as a matter of routine could be accompanied by an intimation from the King that the attendance of the person named in it was not desired, and the precedent thus set was revived by Charles I. But in general the composition of the mediaeval House of Lords is of no great significance in the country's constitutional development because the leading nobles killed one another off in the Wars of the Roses. Henry VII's House of Lords had a substantial majority of ecclesiastics. This disappeared at the time of the Reformation, one of whose incidents was the exclusion of the mitred abbots from Parliament. The number of ecclesiastical peers was eventually fixed at twenty-six, at which figure it has since remained despite the creation of new bishoprics. An attempt to limit the number of lay peers was made in George I's reign, but was unsuccessful.

The lay peerage remained small throughout the Tudor period, numbering about sixty at the end of Elizabeth's reign, and during the next century new creations were by no means numerous. But the first half of the eighteenth century, the age of the great landowners, saw new creations on a considerable scale, including a fine crop of new dukedoms, and this was the body of hereditary territorial aristocrats which controlled the House of Commons through pocket boroughs. Pitt considerably altered the composition of the House of Lords by advising the Crown to award peerages to rich merchants, and in his day the House first assumed the form that it has since retained of an assembly of men who have inherited both position and wealth. The new creations did not at first alter the balance of political power, Pitt's repeated attempts at reform all breaking down, and the place of the House of Lords in the constitution was not seriously affected until 1832. The gradual decline in the powers of the House of Lords continued through the nineteenth century and was eventually accelerated by the fact that Mr. Gladstone's adoption of the policy of Home Rule for Ireland drove many Liberal peers into the Conservative camp and gave the House its one-sided party complexion. When a Liberal Government was returned to power in 1906 with an immense majority in the House of Commons, conflict with the Lords was inevitable. It culminated in the passage of the Parliament Act of 1911, which permits the House of Lords to delay a Bill for two years, unless it is a Money Bill, when the period is reduced to one month. At the expiry of the stated time the Bill can receive the Royal assent without the House of Lords having consented to its passage.

The preamble to the Parliament Act stated that it was intended to reconstitute the House of Lords on a popular instead of a hereditary basis, but no steps have been taken to implement this undertaking. There has been no need to take them because the present arrangement has worked smoothly. This development, which was hardly expected when the Parliament Bill became law, is due partly to the fact that in the 34 years between the passage of the Parliament Act and the return of the Labour Party to power, no new subjects of acute political controversy presented themselves, and partly to the fact that at least three-quarters of the members of the House of Lords do not act upon their writs of summons. The House of Lords as it actually functions is a small body including many men of personal distinction, able to ventilate issues of public interest with which the House of Commons has no time to deal at length. It remains, however, a predominantly Conservative body and is therefore not as effective as it might be. When circumstances convince the English people that they need a second chamber of a kind that Americans would describe as having teeth in it, the House of Lords will be reconstructed, and reconstruction will then be facilitated by the fact that the mass of hereditary peers have ceased to attend.[1]

THERE is, of course, no hereditary element anywhere in the American Constitution, and though a few names have persisted on the senatorial roll for long periods, the strength of the Senate resides in the fact that, under a federal Constitution, its members represent the States. But by one of the little paradoxes in which history delights, this source of strength is also a source of weakness because every State of the Union is represented by two senators, Nevada, with a population of about one hundred thousand, having the same representation as New York with a population of some thirteen million. Americans who wish to reform the Senate are tempted to remodel the boundaries of States and more particularly to raise the

---

[1] A Bill placed before the House of Commons in January 1948 would curtail the Lords' power by further restricting the period by which a Bill may be delayed, from two years to one.

great urban areas, such as New York and Chicago
with their large populations, to the dignity of State-
hood. One great change in the Senate's constitution
has actually been made. Until 1913 the members of
the Senate were elected by the State legislatures. In
that year the seventeenth amendment to the Constitution transferred election to the people. The change
was not so great as it would appear because the system
of voting the ticket meant that members of the State
legislatures were in most cases returned already
pledged to elect as Senators the persons chosen by the
direct primary or imposed upon it by the local party
managers.

The seventeenth amendment had no effect on the
powers entrusted to the Senate by the Constitution.
Ample though they are, they are smaller than were
first conferred by the Philadelphia Convention. The
first draft of the Constitution gave the Senate the appointment of ambassadors and judges as well as
the negotiation of treaties, and the question whether the
President should be elected by the Senate or by the
House—no one advocated direct election by the people—was left open until the convention had reached
its final stage. In legislation the two Houses have
equal powers. It is true that Money Bills have to
originate in the House, but as the Senate can and does
amend them in such a way as to transform their character this provision is of little practical importance.
Except in the case of Money Bills it is quite usual for
the House and the Senate to be dealing at the same
time with the same subject, each Chamber having its

own Bill,[2] an arrangement that the course of constitutional development has made impossible in England. In the Tudor and Stuart periods, when the two English Houses were roughly equal in power and when each could completely veto the proceedings of the other, conferences between their members to adjust differences of opinion were part of the regular constitutional procedure. They have since become obsolete in England because the eighteenth century House of Lords dominated the House of Commons and the nineteenth century House of Commons could usually impose its will on the House of Lords. In the United States these conferences between delegations from the two Houses are regularly held because they are indispensable to the effective working of the constitution. Without a conference it would hardly be possible for any Bill of importance to be passed.

It would seem that the framers of the Constitution, who knew their English history and were determined to avoid autocracy in government, had present to their minds some analogy between the President and the mediaeval King working with a body of councillors. The Senate as originally constituted could not have numbered more than twenty-six and in fact numbered only twenty-two. It was therefore of a size to serve as a council, and it appears significant in this connection that the Constitution makes no mention of a Cabinet. Washington called his depart-

---

[2] This is why American legislation is often referred to by the names of its two parents, the one a Senator and the other a Representative—for example, the Hawley-Smoot Tariff, or the Taft-Hartley Labor Act.

I

mental heads into consultation, his successors have
followed his example and English precedent has
caused the name Cabinet to be applied to the group
thus formed. But its meetings are a matter of usage
only and no President is under any constitutional obligation either to appoint a Cabinet or to call its members together. It was definitely intended that the
President should work with the Senate in the matter
of public appointments. All important appointments
require senatorial approval, and Englishmen discovered with some surprise during the recent war that
the Senate's consent is required to promotions in the
higher ranks of the Army. The President's nominations to the bench of the Supreme Court and to places
in his own Cabinet require the Senate's consent before
they can become effective, and this consent is by no
means a matter of course. As recently as President
Coolidge's day a Cabinet nomination was rejected by
the Senate, and the Supreme Court has been a battle-
ground between President and Senate in the past and
may possibly become one again in the future. When
a nomination is submitted to the Senate it is referred
to a committee which, if the majority in the Senate—
and hence of the committee—is hostile to the President, may not report for a considerable time. When
it reports, its recommendation is considered by the
Senate in what is called executive session. The Senate's rules exclude the public from such a session, but
though the doors of the Chamber are nominally
closed somebody is always listening at the key-hole.
The general procedure in the matter of appointments,

which nowadays run into many thousands, has been settled by usage. Federal appointments of national importance are dealt with by the Senate as a whole. Appointments geographically and politically associated with localities and within states are referred to one or both of the Senators of the State concerned if they are of the President's party, and are agreed to by what is called the courtesy of the Senate. On the other hand, the veto of the Senator to whom the nomination has been referred is absolute; it is on record that a Senator once objected to a man on the ground that he was "personally obnoxious" and that the Senate sustained his objection. In cases where neither of the Senators of a State is of the President's party, all appointments within states are referred to the State's delegation in the House of Representatives, who are normally consulted about minor appointments in their particular districts. When there are no Representatives to consult, as happens in all the Southern States when a Republican President is in office, appointments are referred to the State Committee of the majority party.

There is only one expedient by which a President can be reasonably certain of getting the immediate consent of a possibly hostile Senate to his nomination to a major post and that is for him to nominate a Senator. Here the courtesy of the Senate operates to prevent enquiry by a committee. The Senate regards all its members as of equal standing, though in fact some of the worst as well as some of the best figures in American politics have sought and obtained senatorial

seats. Now that the previous balance of the American
Constitution has been impaired by the breach of the
convention that a President shall not serve more than
two terms, the fact that the Senate has effective control over the great appointments and that it does not
exercise that control when an appointment is offered
to one of its own members may become of constitutional importance.[3]

Appointments are among the most important functions of the executive Government, and in this field,
notwithstanding the doctrine of the separation of
powers, there is a partnership between the holder of
executive power and a branch of the legislature. It
is a partnership of a peculiar kind in that the Senate
can suggest nobody but can veto anybody, and by
making it clear that it is prepared to use its powers
can force Presidents to play for safety. It thus can
present itself as a constitutional watch-dog exercising
over persons the same sort of authority as the Supreme
Court exercises over laws and it has two methods of
keeping this aspect of its functions well before the
public mind. It appoints strong and zealous committees to investigate scandals and, while members
of the House refer to the President with the respect
due to the Head of the State, the Senate meets him

---

[3] A constitutional amendment limiting the Presidential terms to
two was proposed by Congress and submitted to the States for
ratification in March 1947. To date the legislatures of twenty-one
States have ratified the amendment, which is still fifteen short of
the necessary number to make the amendment a part of the Constitution. Under the terms of the Congressional proposal, ratification must be accomplished by March 1954, or the amendment will
be considered lost.

on the level. To an angry Senator of the opposite
party the President is "that man in the White House,"
whose acts may be described in language going beyond any that a British Prime Minister would use
about an intractable colleague after his resignation.
On the other hand, a strong President can bring the
Senate to heel. President Hoover put some pressure
on it to pass legislation. President Woodrow Wilson
went much further. When a measure was held up in
the Senate by the form of persistent obstruction
known as a filibuster, the President issued from the
White House a public denunciation so scathing that
the Senate felt obliged to pass a closure rule. Its application, however, remains exceptional and prob-
lematical.

But the outstanding feature of the Senate's powers
is its position with regard to the conclusion of treaties.
Under the American Constitution a treaty is not submitted to the House of Representatives. It is submitted only to the Senate, and to become effective
must obtain a two-thirds vote of those present. There
are ninety-six members of the Senate, and forty-nine
of them constitute a quorum. Seventeen hostile votes
can therefore prevent a two-thirds majority being
obtained, or defeat a treaty; and these seventeen could
come from States that contained only about one-
twelfth of the country's population—according to the
1940 census rather more than ten million inhabitants,
or three million fewer than the State of New York
at the head of the list. If the figures for Pennsylvania
and Illinois, the States which for long immediately

followed New York,[4] be added to the New York total, the sum exceeds thirty millions, nearly a quarter of the entire population of the United States. But though the three great States can decide Presidential elections and settle the political colour of the House of Representatives, they have only six votes in the Senate and constitute but one-sixteenth of its strength. They are therefore equally unable to veto a treaty or to guarantee its passage.

The two-thirds rule worked satisfactorily so long as the United States could pursue a general policy of isolationism, the small States whose combination could wreck a treaty being as a rule just those States most limited in their outlook. Whether the two-thirds rule can hold now that the United States is becoming permanently committed to a leading part in world affairs is a question already being discussed. The rule can be changed only by the slow process of constitutional amendment, and, stated in constitutional terms, the case for change is that the rule has never worked very well. For example, a treaty may require a money vote to make its provisions effective, but a Money Bill must originate in the House of Representatives, and this tends to stimy the purported authority of the Senate (as, e.g., in the deliberations on the European Recovery Program). Again, the two-thirds rule may be evaded, and that in the most important matters, by avoiding the form of a treaty. A hundred years ago a treaty admitting the then independent State of Texas

---

[4] According to the latest figures California has displaced Illinois in the population table.

into the Union failed to get two-thirds support in the Senate. Texas was then admitted by resolutions of both Houses, which could be carried by a simple majority. Alternatively, the method of direct executive action can be adopted. It was by such action that Jefferson in 1803-4 carried through the Louisiana Purchase, which nearly doubled the territorial area of the United States. Jefferson himself was of the opinion that a constitutional amendment was needed to validate his action, but was advised that the amendment might not be ratified. He therefore did not seek a constitutional amendment. His conduct supplied a precedent to Franklin Roosevelt when he acquired bases for the United States in British territory by executive action alone. Thus the power of the President to conclude Executive Agreements has been established—a power which brings the President's powers very near the prerogative of the Crown in the matter of treaty-making. That this was far from the intention of the framers of the Constitution will be demonstrated further on.

That the powers of executive and legislature in international matters will need to be defined afresh is more than a possibility. The question has, indeed, already arisen in connection with commitments which the United States has accepted as a member of the United Nations and may be called upon to implement in the future. Is action, and especially military action, "to maintain or restore international peace and security" (U.N. Charter, Art. 39ff.) to be taken on the authority of the President alone? Or will the consent of two-thirds of the Senators present be required in cases of action involving the use of United States armed forces? Or is such action to be regarded as a declaration of war on the offender and therefore needing approval by a majority in both Houses? Forty years ago it proved impossible to conclude treaties of arbitration that were general in more than name because the Senate insisted upon its right to decide whether each particular issue as it arose should be regarded as arbitrable. But opinion in the United States, and in the Senate itself, has moved a long way since John Hay, who was Theodore Roosevelt's Secretary of State, sadly compared a treaty submitted to the Senate to a doomed bull entering the arena.

This is one of the few points in the allocation of powers in which the English tradition could give no guidance and English precedents no help. Under the English constitution the treaty-making power is vested in the Crown, subject, of course, to the qualifications that the Crown can neither spend money nor cede territory without the consent of Parliament. Developments very easily might have taken a different course. Because of the weakness of their title, the Lancastrian Kings were always anxious to secure the support of Parliament, and in 1420 Henry V concluded a most important treaty upon whose provisions some consultation with the English people was obviously desirable. This was the Treaty of Troyes, which provided that the King of England should become immediate Regent and prospective King of France, and so affected the whole position of the dynasty. The Treaty was therefore made subject to Parliamentary approval and late in the century Henry VII, whose title was also weak, thought it well to revive the Lancastrian precedent. But when his son sought legislative approval for a scale of import duties, Parliament jibbed. It was part of the House of Commons tradition that members must stick to their proper business and not weaken their position by dealing with matters that were too great for them. In this instance Parliament took the ground, which modern economists might dispute, that import duties would be paid by foreigners and that its concern was only with Englishmen. Its action proved decisive. Henry VIII himself was always respectful of Parliamentary feeling. But Elizabeth, and still more the Stuarts, were in no mood to submit to Parliament matters that were admitted to lie within the competence of the royal prerogative. At the time of the Revolution it would have been theoretically easy for Parliament to stipulate that it should be consulted between the conclusion of a treaty and its ratification, but any such course was practically impossible. William III stood below his wife in the line of succession but was not prepared to come to England simply as Mary's husband nor to wear the Crown unless he were given freedom of action in the conduct of international affairs. It has thus come about that the treaty-making power has remained intact in the hands of the Crown, which to-day means in the hands of the Cabinet.

In recent times the House of Commons has shown some restiveness under this arrangement. With the country at peace it would probably be impossible for the Government to conclude an important treaty without consulting Parliament, and as the Cabinet is well aware of its dependence on the House of Commons, it is normally ready to grant time for the discussion of a treaty whose terms have aroused public interest, even though no formal parliamentary sanction be requisite. But in time of war the treaty-making power of the Crown is a most valuable instrument. It enables treaties to be negotiated, signed and brought into force with the necessary secrecy. The treaty of alliance with Italy in the 1914 war, the treaty of alliance with Poland shortly before the outbreak of hostilities in 1939, and the long-term treaty of alliance with Russia in 1941 are all examples of commitments profoundingly affecting the country's policy that were undertaken on the assumption that Parliament would approve of them but for which no actual expression of parliamentary approval was obtained.

The American President has no powers (though see above the actions of Jefferson and Franklin Roosevelt concerning respectively the Louisiana Purchase and the West Indian bases) in any way corresponding to those enjoyed by the English King, and any conferment of them was out of the question from the first. Having got rid of an autocratic government seated overseas, the Americans were at all possible pains to avoid establishing anything of the sort at home, and the Philadelphia Convention had no difficulty in deciding that the principle of the separation of powers must for once be abandoned and the legisla-

ture in some way associated with the executive in
the conclusion of treaties. No sentence in the Constitution has been more thoroughly canvassed than
that which sets out the arrangement actually concluded. It runs: "He (the President) shall have power
by and with the advice and consent of the Senate,
to make treaties, provided two-thirds of the Senators
present concur; and he shall nominate, and, by and
with the advice and consent of the Senate, shall appoint ambassadors, other public ministers and consuls,
judges of the Supreme Court, and all other officers of
the United States, whose appointments are not herein
otherwise provided for, and which shall be established
by law." What exactly is implied in the words "make
treaties"? It will be noted that in the latter part of
the sentence the order of the words indicates that
the President is to nominate ambassadors, judges and
other officials on his own motion, but that the advice
and consent of the Senate is required to validate their
appointments. Even here it is not quite clear in what
way the Senate can give advice, as opposed to consent
or refusal, when a name is once laid before it. But the
first part of the sentence is more obscure still. The
making of a treaty involves two stages: its negotiation
and its subsequent consideration when the text has
been agreed upon; and in the language of the Constitution, these two stages are run into one.

There is, however, little doubt about what the
authors of the Constitution intended. While its ratification by the States was still in debate there were
published in New York, first in the Press and later in

book form under the general title of *The Federalist*, a series of eighty-five papers all signed "Publius" but actually written by Alexander Hamilton, James Madison and John Jay, the two former sometimes collaborating. Of these three writers, Madison attended the Convention's sittings throughout and probably had a greater influence than any other member in guiding its deliberations. Hamilton was present at the start but withdrew when he found that his views were unpopular, though he returned in time to sign the Constitution. Jay was not a member of the Convention but was in charge of the Foreign Affairs department of the Congress and the few papers which he contributed all are concerned with his special subject. From the date of their appearance the *Federalist* papers have been accepted as an authoritative commentary on the Constitution. In regard to the restriction of the treaty-making power to the Senate, the *Federalist* explains that the popular house, which was planned to consist of sixty-five members, was rendered incapable by its size of conducting international business with the necessary secrecy and despatch, but that this function could properly be performed by the Senate, which numbered only twenty-two (*Federalist* No. 64 (Jay); No. 75 (Hamilton). This language implies that the Senate should be associated with the President in the negotiation of treaties. An attempt at such association was actually made by Washington, who brought the draft of an Indian treaty to the Senate in order to go through it with its members; but the Senators felt they could not deliberate in comfort in the President's presence and to Washington's outspoken annoyance referred the treaty to a committee. In later years Washington consulted the Senate from time to time about the principles of policy that should guide American negotiators, and such consultation has continued intermittently ever since, a recent instance occurring when President Truman enlisted Senatorial aid in negotiating peace treaties. But after Washington's initial failure, no President personally brought a treaty to the Senate until President Wilson came to the Chamber, bringing the Treaty of Versailles and offering his assistance, which was not accepted, in its consideration.

The general principles governing the relation of the Senate with the President in regard to treaties were laid down by a Resolution of the Senate as early as 1816 and have been adhered to ever since. The Senate feels that it can take no part in the negotiation of a treaty; that is the business of the Executive to which American ambassadors and others concerned in negotiation are responsible. The functions of the Senate begin when the text of an agreed treaty is laid before it. The Senate then can accept or reject a treaty forthwith. But the usual procedure is to refer a treaty to the Committee on Foreign Relations, where, if opposition develops, it may remain for years as actually happened in the case of the Treaty of Alliance with Britain and France that President Wilson negotiated after the First World War and that, having been duly referred to the Committee, still awaits its consideration. The advice and consent

formula clearly implies a right on the part of the
Senate to amend the text of the treaty, and this right
has on occasion been exercised; but the Senate has no
means of compelling the President to do, in a positive
sense, what it wishes him to do. The doctrine of the
separation of powers has rendered President and Congress as independent of one another as were Crown
and Parliament in Tudor and Stuart England. Still
less, of course, has the Senate any means of inducing
the foreign party to the treaty to accept Senatorial
amendments or even of bringing them to its notice.
There has therefore been evolved the device of reservations. A reservation does not touch the text of a
treaty but it explains what the Senate understands
this text to mean and makes it clear that if the treaty
is accepted at all, it will be accepted only on the understanding that its text is to be interpreted by the United
States in the Senate's sense. In practice the relation
of reservations to text are occasionally remote. The
Senate's proposed reservations to the Treaty of Versailles included one in favour of Home Rule for Ireland, a subject to which the text of the Treaty makes
no reference; but by the time this reservation was
adopted it was becoming clear that the Treaty would
not go through and the adoption of the reservation
was merely a political manoeuvre.

The provision that a treaty must be accepted by
two-thirds of the Senators present, which means that
in the Senate as at present constituted the opposition
of thirty-four votes makes the defeat of a treaty cer-

tain, is apparently the result of the first major piece of log-rolling in American constitutional history. The six southern States were concerned lest the seven northern States should seek to abolish the slave traffic. This would need to be done by treaty, and the South, not content with the proviso in the Constitution that the issue of slavery should not in any case be touched for twenty years, was not prepared to allow any such treaty to be concluded by a bare majority. The two-thirds requirement made it certain that no treaty affecting the slave traffic could become law without the consent of at least some of the slave States. In return the northern States secured the power to pass by ordinary legislation tariffs protecting American manufacturers, upon which the South, which imported most of its finished products, had looked with no favourable eye. Slavery has long since vanished from the United States but a treaty requirement originally devised to maintain that institution still remains. The Senate has now grown to a size that makes it even more incapable of secrecy and despatch than was the House of Representatives of the First Congress, and the argument that the Senate is less susceptible to the tumults of popular opinion has long since lost much of its force, thanks both to the development of American methods of publicity and to the transfer of the choice of Senators from the State legislatures to the electorate. Treaties nevertheless still lie exclusively within the Senate's province. This remains so although the power of the President to conclude Executive Agreements has been so en-larged in the course of developments that through it many matters can be settled which, from a more orthodox viewpoint, might be considered as proper subjects for treaties.

COMMONS AND REPRESENTATIVES

LTHOUGH the American Senate surpasses the British House of Lords in power and value, by way of compensation the British House of Commons holds a place in the Constitution to which the American House of Representatives cannot hope to aspire. This place is due first to the Commons' assertion of control over the public purse, and secondly to its use of that control in such a way as to make the executive Government dependent upon its confidence. Both these sources of the Commons' power were acquired almost accidently. The great desire of the early Parliaments was that the King should live of his own, that is to say, should conduct the business of Government out of the revenues assigned to him for life at the beginning of his reign. These revenues, however, would not provide the sinews of war and Parliaments were called together to place at the King's disposal the necessary funds, which were derived from a rudimentary system of direct taxation. It thus came about that the frequency of Parliaments was directly related to the frequency of wars. No English Sovereign was more persistently belligerent than was Edward III, who held forty-

eight Parliaments during fifty years of his reign (1327-1377). It is from this period that the notion that Parliament should meet frequently and regularly began to take root; but the earliest Parliament whose sessions were sufficiently continuous and prolonged for Members to get to know one another and to acquire a real sense of corporate unity was the Reformation Parliament of Henry VIII, which sat for over six years. Elizabeth disliked Parliaments and hurried them through their business, and in the Stuart period the Long Parliament itself, by which the constitutional supremacy of Parliaments was first asserted, was so little prepared to contemplate the House of Commons as the constantly operating part of the constitutional machine that its own proposals to Cromwell elaborated the provision in the Instrument of Government that Parliaments should be summoned at no longer interval than three years. It was the limitation of the grant of supply to one year after the Revolution that made it necessary for the House of Commons to meet annually.

The further step, the subordination of the executive to the House, followed, as has already been explained, from the impossibility of the Crown's providing itself with Ministers who are not all members of the same Party. Nevertheless Ministers remained the King's Ministers and long felt the King's confidence to be no less necessary than that of the House of Commons. In 1834 William IV of his own motion dismissed the Ministry that had carried the Reform Bill, although it had not been defeated in the House; and as late as

1851, Queen Victoria demanded and obtained the dismissal of Palmerston, because, as Foreign Secretary, he had not kept her properly informed about matters in which she considered it her constitutional duty to take an active interest. To the end of her reign it was felt that the Foreign Secretaryship was a post that could not be filled without the Queen's explicit approval. With this qualification and with some further allowance for the Queen's strong personal dislikes, the constitutional position during her reign was that Cabinet offices were alloted by the Prime Minister and that popular language was correct in speaking of the Queen's Government but of Mr. Gladstone's or Mr. Disraeli's Administration.

The Queen did, however, make some claim to decide who should be Prime Minister. When the Conservative Party was defeated at the polls in 1880, she sent for both Lord Granville and Lord Hartington, the Liberal leaders in both Houses, before she could bring herself to recognise the patent fact that a victorious Liberal Party would have no leader except Mr. Gladstone. Even the Queen, however, was accustomed to ask a resigning Prime Minister whom he would advise her to send for. When Mr. Gladstone finally retired, her dislike of him caused her to break with this practice and she herself sent for Lord Rosebery, though it is understood that had Mr. Gladstone been consulted he would have advised Lord Spencer. The latest example of the choice of a Prime Minister by the Crown occurred as recently as 1923. In that year Mr. Bonar Law, who had been head of the Gov-

ernment for a few months, returned from a continental holiday a dying man and tendered his
resignation to the King by letter without seeking a
farewell audience. Lord Curzon was the most distinguished member of the Government and the leader
of the House of Lords and he not unnaturally expected the premiership. But the official opposition
was then represented by the Labour Party, almost the
whole of whose political strength lay in the Commons.
In these circumstances King George V was doubtful
whether the office of Prime Minister could be given
to a peer. Lord Balfour, the most experienced of the
country's elder statesmen and by then himself somewhat detached from party politics, was consulted and
advised that it could not. The King accordingly sent
for Mr. Baldwin, who was able to form a government.

Neither in the choice of a Prime Minister nor in
the construction of the Cabinet has the House of
Commons, as such, any voice whatever; but party
leaders are elected by the members of the party in
both Houses and at such elections the choice of the
Commons is decisive. Moreover, the sort of reputa-
tion that entitles a politician to a place in the Cabinet
is more easily and more frequently made in the House
of Commons than in the House of Lords or on the
platform. Under the American system members of
the Cabinet are appointed by the President and are
responsible to him. Their appointments need confirmation by the Senate but do not concern the House of
Representatives.

The rise of the House of Commons dates from 1485,

when the destruction of the mediaeval peerage in the
Wars of the Roses left it as the chief organ of public
opinion. Henry VIII was at great pains to carry it
with him in all he did and it is during his reign that
the eldest sons of the new peers of Tudor creation
begin to stand for the House of Commons—first heralds of the crowds of bearers of good county names
who were to fill its benches some two centuries later.
At the accession of the boy King Edward VI in 1547
the House of Commons moved across the road from
the Chapter House at Westminster to the Palace opposite, where accommodation was found for it in St.
Stephen's Chapel. In that year, too, the House first
began to keep the regular journal of its proceedings.

The link between both Houses of Parliament and
the Crown was provided by their presiding officers.
The Lord Chancellor, who conducts the proceedings
of the House of Lords, has never been the choice of
the House but is always nominated by the Crown.
The woolsack [1] is not technically within the House of

---

[1] The woolsack is a broad, cushioned seat immediately in front
of the throne occupied by the Lord Chancellor. In mediaeval
times the Lord Chancellor was the King's chief administrative
officer and attended the sittings of the House of Lords in order
to report its proceedings to his master. The export duty on wool
was the principal source of the revenues on which the King was
expected to live and by a happy and characteristic piece of sym-
bolism his Chancellor's seat was stuffed with that material. The
name remained though the practice was dropped, possibly when
the present Houses of Parliament were built in Queen Victoria's
reign, and until recently the Woolsack was stuffed with horsehair.
In 1938 however, at the insistence of the Wool Secretariat, the
tradition was revived and, in characteristic British fashion, enlarged.
The Lord Chancellor now sits upon a woolsack stuffed with a
blend of British and Dominion wools.

Lords and the Lord Chancellor need not be a peer. The convention by which a peerage is invariably conferred upon him on his appointment dates from early Stuart times. The Commons, who withdrew from the King's presence to consider his requests for money, naturally chose their own Speaker or spokesman to convey their reply, but no less naturally sought the King's approval of their choice, with the consequence that, as the place of the House in the Constitution became more definite, the position of the Speaker tended to approximate more and more that of a Crown official. It is true that on presenting himself after his election for the Crown's approval the Speaker claimed the privilege of free speech for himself. (It was not until Henry VIII's time that the claim was extended to cover all members of the House.) But the Speaker also looked to the Crown for instructions about the business of the House and in the later years of Elizabeth's reign it frequently happened that the Speaker advised the House that the Queen regarded some particular matter as lying outside its province. The crisis came in 1629. Charles I, having made up his mind to govern without a Parliament, instructed Speaker Finch to adjourn the House as a preliminary to its dissolution. The House, however, was not prepared to adjourn until it had clearly stated its position against the Crown. The unfortunate Speaker frankly avowed his difficulty, with his duty to the House clashing with his duty to the Crown. In the end his balance inclined towards the Crown, whereupon members held him down in the Chair until the House had passed its resolutions. The lesson was not lost upon his successor. When Charles I came down to the House in 1641 to arrest five members of the opposition and asked Speaker Lenthall where they were, the Speaker fell on his knees before the King and told him that he had neither eyes to see nor ears to hear except as the House should be pleased to direct him.

For the last three centuries the Speaker has been the servant of the House of Commons and through the wholeheartedness of his service has become its master —the custodian of its traditions, the interpreter of its rules, the protector of the rights of minorities, the one wholly impartial figure in a partisan assembly. It is still the custom of a majority party to fill a vacancy in the Chair from its own ranks but the Opposition is consulted and election now-a-days is unanimous. Once elected the Speaker retains his position during his own pleasure whatever changes there may be in the party complexion of the House.[2]

The position of the Speaker of the House of Representatives is very different. There is no Treasury

---

[2] This implies, of course, that the Speaker retains his seat in the House. Indeed, the Speaker's seat has by long usage been considered inviolable. He is not expected to put up a fight for his constituency because having been elected Speaker he is considered above party. Only once in modern times has the Speaker been opposed in his constituency, namely during the General Election of 1935. At that time Mr. Speaker FitzRoy took no part in the election campaign, but other prominent politicians of various parties fought for him so that he was returned with a great majority. He took his seat as Speaker in the new House amid the acclamations of members of all parties, and it was felt that the usage had been signally vindicated.

Bench in either House of Congress and the conduct of what in England would be called government business raises problems that became acute directly after the Civil War and still await full solution. In the later 1860s Congress, and more particularly the House of Representatives, began to reclaim for itself powers that during the war had passed into the hands of the President as Commander-in-Chief. When Woodrow Wilson wrote his *Congressional Government* in the early 1880s, he took it as a matter of course that the legislature was the dominant element in the Constitution and the substance of his argument was that its government was irresponsible. It is curious that so severe a critic of American institutions should have become President of the United States but perhaps less curious that he should have carried further that re-transfer of power from the Capitol to the White House that had begun under Theodore Roosevelt if not under McKinley.

In the later 1860s President and Congress were at variance over the treatment of Confederate States. In Lincoln's view, which his successor sought to uphold, the Confederate States had never ceased to be members of the Union though certain disloyal persons had obtained control of their governments. In the view of the majority of the House of Representatives, however, the Southern States were rebels lying at the mercy of their conquerors. This view prevailed and the man who took the lead in giving it expression, Thaddeus Stevens, used his position as Chairman of the Ways and Means and Appropriations Committees

to become what English political language would describe as the Leader of the House. The rules of the
House of Representatives, like the rules of the House
of Commons, respected the rights of minorities in debate and so favored obstruction. With the return of
embittered Southerners to Congress in the later phase
of the Reconstruction period, obstruction developed,
a year or so before the Irish party organised it in the
House of Commons.

In England obstruction was dealt with by the Government, though when it first reached its climax the
Speaker acted on his own initiative in adjourning the
House without putting the question. In the United
States it ·was dealt with by a succession of Speakers
acting in concert with the majority. The strongest
and best known of these Speakers was Mr. Cannon,
who held office through a number of Congresses at
the beginning of the century. Speaker Cannon's
power was three-fold; he made appointments to the
principal Committees of the House, he was himself a
member of the Committee of Rules, which controlled
procedure, and he standardised the practice of refus-
ing to recognise members who sought to prolong debate. Yet even at the height of his power he did not
exercise that same undisputed control of the House
that is wielded by the Speaker of the House of Commons. He could not do so because he was the servant
not of the House but of the dominant party. His rulings were subject to debate and were occasionally de-
bated. In 1910 a revolt broke his power, and today
the exclusion of the Speaker from membership of the

Rules Committee means that ultimate control of procedure is no longer in his hands. He is thus more than ever the servant of the party machine and recognises his position. When Mr. Nicholas Longworth was elected Speaker in 1925, his opening address from the Chair defined his duties as both he and the House conceived them: "I believe it to be the duty of the Speaker, standing squarely on the platform of his party, to assist in so far as he properly can the enactment of legislation in accordance with the declared principles and policies of his party and by the same token to resist the enactment of legislation in violation thereof." So deeply is the tradition of Mr. Speaker's impartiality ingrained in English minds that an Englishman cannot read these words without a shock.

THE fear of mob-law, which did so much to shape the decisions of the Philadelphia Convention, was never more manifest than in its arrangements for the sessions of the House of Representatives. A new House is elected in November every other year, but does not normally meet until the following January. Moreover, until 1933, no person elected on the second Tuesday in November could enter on his duties until the following March 4th. The provision dates from the period when communications were slow and difficult and it is significant of American conservatism in constitutional matters that it was not altered till President Franklin Roosevelt's time and then only to the extent of substituting January 3rd for Senators and Representatives and January 20th for the President and Vice-President.

Until the date of the change-over the old House remains in being. There was thus formerly ample time, and there is still a period of eight weeks, for it to legislate after the election of its successor; and when the elections changed the party majority the American public was treated to the unedifying spectacle of what was known as a "lame duck" session, in which the defeated party set itself to create obstacles in the path of its victorious opponents. Congressmen who had been defeated at the polls but hoped to do better next time would not easily lend themselves to a practice so obnoxious to popular feeling, but one of the points in which the House of Representatives differs from the House of Commons is that party struggles are more unrelenting and less tempered by objective considerations. Besides, the idea that political experience should be spread over as wide a field as possible was established in American minds by Jefferson. Accordingly members of Congress are, on the whole, more inclined to take chances with the electorate or to stake their future on odd political opportunities. Even Lincoln had sat in one House only when he was adopted as his party's candidate for the Presidency.

The House of Representatives labours under many disadvantages. Its life is short; a large proportion of its members are without political experience; and within a relatively brief span of its statutory meeting its members, their eyes on the constitutional clock, would be thinking of adjournment in order to take part in the new election campaign. Perhaps it is more than an accident of language that makes an Englishman stand for Parliament where an American runs for Congress.

The outstanding feature of the procedure of the House of Representatives as a whole is its subordination to its Committees. There being no Government control over the business of the House, any member can introduce a bill, and as members are always ready to oblige pressure groups or cranks among their constituents, the number of bills introduced into each Congress runs into many thousands. Once introduced, a bill is assigned by the Speaker to its appropriate Committee. The House has now—since adoption of the Reorganization Act of 1946, by which the number of standing committees in both houses was to be reduced by more than half—nineteen standing committees; the Senate with its smaller membership makes shift with fifteen. The most important Committees are regarded as exclusive, that is to say, membership of one of them excludes from membership of any other Committee. Appointments to Committees are made by the party managers, and the composition of the Committees reflects party strength. The most important Committees are constituted at the beginning of each Congress but appointments to the minor Committees are sometimes held up so that expectant nominees may be kept obedient to party discipline until the biggest bill of the session has gone through.

Position in a Committee is determined by seniority, the member of the majority party who has had the longest continuous service on a Committee automatically becoming its chairman. If a member loses his seat and is out of the House for two years he starts again at the bottom of the list. This rule of continuous service means that chairmanships go to the men who have got the safe seats and they would not have the safe seats unless they were thoroughly "sound" Republicans or Democrats as the case may be. The Chairman's power is very considerable; he decides the order in which bills referred to his Committee shall be taken, with the result that a bill not desired by the majority party may not come up for consideration at all. Nevertheless the procedure of Committees is not, on the whole, partisan. In the case of a tariff bill, indeed, partisanship is inevitable and the majority of the members of the Ways and Means Committee meet separately and determine the main lines of the bill without consulting their colleagues. But apart from the tariff, legislative proposals of major importance obtain sufficient support from both parties for their eventual passage into law to be described as bi-partisan. This is one of the most notable points of difference between the British and the American systems. In Britain controversy rages over the chief items in a Government's programme and their progress through the Commons intensifies the lines of party cleavage. In America it is usual for contributions towards the final shape of an important measure to come from both sides of the House and nothing puzzles the British student of American institutions so much as this tendency of party lines to become blurred in the actual passage of legislation. To some extent this difference is due to the separation of powers which is an essential feature of the American constitution. Congress can and does think of itself as a whole, presenting legislation to the President for signature. Allowance must also be made for the greater frequency of elections in the United States, and for the greater part that public opinion is consequently able to play in determining the attitude of parties concerned to retain their full polling strength and not to present votes to their opponents.

This circumstance accounts for the great significance of pressure groups in American politics. They organise public opinion and they operate impartially on both parties in the interests of the cause they have at heart. This, too, is one of the reasons for the difficulty that foreign observers experience in finding the line of political division between the two parties. It is also possible that the need of a three-quarters vote to secure a constitutional amendment, with its implication that thorough-going change calls for the endorsement of the mass of public opinion, exercises an influence over all important legislation, even when admittedly within the four corners of the constitution. In requiring exceptional majorities under certain circumstances the American Constitution departs from British, and indeed from European democratic practice. As this provision affects the conclusion of treaties it looms large in the eyes of foreigners and it may be that they over-estimate its significance for the country's political life.

When a Committee has a bill before it, it sits with open or closed doors, at its discretion. It hears witnesses who are interrogated by its members, and both counsel and Cabinet members can appear before it. When a bill is through Committee it goes back to the House. The more important Committees have priority and can report their measures at any time; also bills introduced at the instigation of the President or of department heads—so-called administration measures—are often given the right of way. Other bills take their place on a list classified by subjects into what are called calendars, and the rules of the House lay down which calendar shall be considered on each day of the week when the House is in session. The most important calendar is that listing bills that are to be taken up by unanimous consent. This does not mean that the subjects are non-contentious; on the contrary, what it means is that both parties are agreed that the subject is one on which both must take their definite stand. Bills reported from a Committee are dealt with under a rigid time limit and only one motion to recommit is in order. The procedure leaves little room for the manoeuvre known in British politics as a snap division, but it is possible to move that the rules be suspended, and if this motion is successful, a Committee can forthwith be discharged from the consideration of a particular bill, and the bill brought up to the House and passed through all its stages in a sitting.

The contrast with English procedure is most

marked. The House of Commons is traditionally reluctant to part with its control over the Committee
stage of Bills. Only the sheer impossibility of getting
through its work reconciled it to the despatch of minor Bills "upstairs," that is to say to committees to
which only a limited number of members were appointed. Until recently there were four Grand Committees (so called to distinguish them from the
Committee on Private Bills and from Select Committees specially appointed) and a Scottish Committee.
Under this procedure the whole House went into
Committee on measures of first class importance, with
the consequence that it was not possible to dispose of
more than one highly controversial measure and of
the Budget in an average session.[3] As the volume
of legislation increased and the opposition resorted to
obstructive tactics, it became necessary to conduct the
committee stage under a time-table. There were thus
evolved the legislative instruments known as the

---

[3] Obviously, the Committee of the Whole in the House of
Representatives plays a somewhat different rôle. As "Committee
of the Whole House on the State of the Union" it handles most
"public" bills as Americans understand this term, that is, those
of general application, irrespective of their origin; indeed, all
revenue and appropriation bills, when first brought up for debate,
must be considered by the Committee of the Whole. But the
function of the Committee is mainly a procedural one, namely
that of ensuring greater informality of discussion than is granted
under the regular rules. As "Committee of the Whole House" the
Committee also considers "private" or "special" bills, that is, those
that apply only to specified persons or places. In some respects,
this may be compared to the Committee on Private Bills in the
House of Commons, although the former again occupies but an
intermediate position between the standing committees and the
House proper.

"guillotine" and the "Kangaroo," the former cutting short discussions of a batch of clauses at a fixed time and the latter enabling the chairman or the Speaker himself (in the report stage) to select amendments for discussion. The Labour Government, on taking office in 1945, cleared the way for its heavy programme by an amendment of the Standing Orders that increased the number of Committees to ten, and thanks to this change even first-class measures are now sent upstairs. The new arrangement is still on trial. It leaves the House uninformed of the details of measures to which it has given a second reading, and the cut in the size of British newspapers owing to the shortage of newsprint means that the politically-minded public is not sufficiently aware of what Parliament is doing.

The beginnings of the procedure under which the whole House was accustomed to go into Committee can be traced back to Tudor times when the Speaker was the servant rather of the Crown than of the House and reported to the Crown what the House was doing. But the House could never have developed its formulation of grievances if it had not been able to conduct its proceedings without the knowledge of the Crown, and in order to maintain the secrecy of its deliberations, it invented the expedient of going into Committee. The Speaker then vacates the Chair and the Mace is removed. The House is constituted without a Speaker and though the Speaker can, if he chooses, remain in the House and listen to

L

the debate, he is no longer an officer of the House, officially aware of what is said and properly equipped to report proceedings to the Crown. Thus the strength of the House of Commons has lain in its power to retain effective control over all legislation submitted to it by the Government, whereas the strength of the House of Representatives resides in its ability to decentralise its business and so handle the immense volume of legislation that reaches it indiscriminately, not principally from the Treasury Bench, which does not exist, but from all and sundry of its 435 members.

The difference between the two procedures is glaring, and yet the methods of the House of Representatives can be parallelled from the House of Commons if search be made in the right place. At every Session the House of Commons has to consider legislation of importance not introduced by the Government; a municipality may seek authority to provide a new water supply, or a railway company to construct a new line. The orthodox procedure is by Private Bill. After its introduction the bill is referred to the Private Bills' Committee, which hears both counsel and witnesses, including, it may be, Ministers, and reports back to the House, which passes the measure, usually without debate, under what Americans would call the unanimous consent rule. In England this procedure, being confined to Private Bills, is a minor part of the activities of the House of Commons. In the United States, where all bills are necessarily private bills (since there are no government or "public" bills in the British sense), it comprehends all the activities of the House of Representatives. So profound is the practical difference effected by the principle of the separation of powers.

THE LAW OF THE LAND

INCE the American Constitution is a written document and since the world does not stand still, the Constitution will from time to time stand in need of interpretation and, if necessary, of amendment. It is now the accepted principle of the American Constitution that interpretation belongs to the Supreme Court, while amendment is the business of the people acting through their representatives both in Congress and in the State legislatures. Experience, endorsing the vigorous initiative of Chief Justice Marshall, has settled with a finality recently shown to be beyond challenge an issue that the Founding Fathers preferred to leave open. The Convention considered and rejected an alternative method—based on French constitutional experience—of associating the President with the judges in the work of constitutional interpretation. The Convention also made the Supreme Court the final Court of Appeal in all litigation arising out of the Constitution and federal legislation, in disputes between States, and in other specified matters. It further declared that the Constitution was the supreme law of the land, and it thus gave po. 'er to the

Supreme Court to set aside any decision of a State Court that could be held to be at variance with the Constitution; but so far as explicitly empowering the Supreme Court to declare an Act of Congress unconstitutional and therefore void, it thrice considered a proposal to this effect and as often decided to take no action.

The assumption of this power by the Supreme Court is no doubt the consequence of the traditional English respect for law as such, but it was by no means an obvious consequence. The whole question was complicated by the universal acceptance at the end of the eighteenth century of the Social Contract theory. What sort of contract was a Constitution? Was it a contract made by the people of the United States to create a new society and a body of law through which that society could function? Or was it a contract made by the peoples of the various States with one another? Or thirdly, was it a contract of a more definitely legal character entered into by the Governments of the various States to transfer certain of their powers to a new authority? At first sight the question is answered by the opening words of the preamble of the Constitution: "We the people of the United States," but it is known that in the original draft the names of the various States were mentioned and were struck out by the Committee on Style, to which the final revision was entrusted, not on account of any theory about the nature of the social contract that they were considering, but on the practical grounds that it was uncertain which of the States

would ratify the Constitution when it was submitted
to them. In the last resort the ambiguity is in the term
United States itself; if the emphasis be put on the
word "United," the United States is a single entity;
if the emphasis be put on the word "States," it is an
association of distinct bodies.[1] The former view has
of course prevailed since the Civil War, but it was by
no means orthodox when the Constitution was
drafted. On the contrary, there is no point on which
the *Federalist* papers insist more strongly than that
"it will always be far more easy for the State Governments to encroach upon the national authorities than
for the national government to encroach upon the
State authorities." (*Federalist*, No. 17 (Hamilton);
Federalist, No. 31 (Hamilton); *Federalist*, No. 46
(Madison).)

Argument on these lines implies that the national
government had no more authority than the States
had delegated to it. It is true that elsewhere Hamilton
declares in his rhetorical way that "the fabric of
American Empire ought to rest on the solid basis of
THE CONSENT OF THE PEOPLE" (*Federalist*, No. 22).
But there is no doubt whatever about the meaning that the Philadelphia Convention attached to
the consent of the people. The ratification of the
Constitution was to be sought not from the people
of the United States as a whole but from the peoples
of the thirteen States expressing their views through

---

[1] The ambiguity conveniently evades the awkward question of
the location of sovereignty and, because of its convenience, has
been perpetuated in the term "United Nations."

conventions. Apparently, however, the difficulty was
felt in the first years of the Constitution and the tenth
amendment, which was passed before the eighteenth
century was out, sought to dispose of the question by
leaving it open. This amendment declares that "the
powers not delegated to the United States by the
Constitution, nor prohibited by it to the States, are reserved to the States respectively, or to the people."
Possibly this amendment may itself one day stand in
need of judicial interpretation, but at present it would
certainly appear that the Constitution knows nothing
of the people of the United States as a whole. Presidents are elected and constitutional amendments ratified or rejected by the people voting by States. In so
far, then, as the Constitution is a social contract, it
was concluded by the peoples of the original thirteen
States and adhered to by the people of subsequent
States as they were created.

But it also can be claimed that the Constitution is
a legal contract that the governments of the States received the authority of their electorates to conclude,
and this was the line actually taken in the resolutions
of protest, which came very near to defiance, passed
in the 1790s by Kentucky and Virginia when Congress passed Acts of which these States disapproved
and by which they claimed they were not bound except by their consent. It is noteworthy in this connection that the Virginian Resolution was drafted by
Madison himself. (Jefferson, who was responsible for
the Kentucky Resolution, was not a member of the
Convention.) The issue was not pressed at the time

but it contained the germs of the Civil War. If in the last resort a State is indeed a sovereign Commonwealth, then it has a right to withdraw from a Union whose policy it feels unable to endorse. On the face of it the States had a poor case. The Articles of Confederation laid it down that the Union should be perpetual (Art. 13) and the Constitution that superseded the Articles declared in its preamble that the first of the purposes for which it had been ordained and established was to form a more perfect Union. Going even beyond this, Lincoln held that the Union created the States, as until it was formed they were merely colonies; but the conception of sovereign Commonwealths delegating authority to a central body which is explicit in the Articles of Confederation did not altogether fade from men's minds, and if the States were indeed sovereign, then it was within their right to interpret the powers that they had bestowed.

It might also be contended that the right of interpretation was vested in the President. In the oath that the second Article of the Constitution imposes on the President when taking office he declares that he will to the best of his ability preserve, protect and defend it. How can a President preserve the Constitution unless he knows what it is, and does not the qualifying reference to the best of his ability imply that he is to exercise his discretion in deciding what is constitutional and what is not? This was the line at least indicated by Andrew Jackson, who, when he was dissatisfied with a judgement of the Supreme Court said, "John Marshall has given his decision; let him enforce it." Since the separation of powers means in practice that executive, legislature and judiciary is each supreme in its respective sphere but has no means of forcing its will upon the others, rigid application of Jackson's doctrine would bring the government of the United States to a standstill by placing its various organs in frank opposition to one another.

To avoid such a dangerous development the challenge to the Supreme Court has in practice taken a different form. If the executive—it is the executive rather than the legislature that has felt outraged by Supreme Court decisions—finds itself confronted by a hostile Supreme Court, the situation can be saved by a change in the personnel of the Court. This is in fact what happened in Grant's day when two vacancies in the court were hurriedly filled and favourable decisions on reconstruction legislation were obtained by the resultant conversion of a dissenting judgement into a majority opinion; and the balance of voices would have similarly been swung over in President Franklin Roosevelt's day if the President had got what he wanted. President Roosevelt offered himself for re-election in 1936 on the strength of his New Deal legislation. He was triumphantly re-elected, carrying 46 out of the 48 States of the Union. In face of this manifestation of popular feeling, the Supreme Court ruled that some of the principal items of his legislation were unconstitutional. The President was angry and proposed, by fixing an age for retirement and increasing the Court's numbers, to create a new majority sympathetic to his policies. But the President had overestimated his popularity. Such is the reverence of the American public for the Supreme Court as an institution that the President was compelled to drop his proposals in view of the hostility that they evoked.

Nevertheless the President in fact got his way in the end and got it through his successful breach of the convention dating from Washington's time that a President shall not be eligible for re-election more than once. Justices of the Supreme Court are naturally fairly advanced in years at the time of their appointment. A President who holds office for four years only may expect to fill one or two vacancies. A President who holds office for eight years may before the expiry of his double term have appointed a majority of the Court; and a President who holds office for twelve years is almost certain to have done so. The prolongation of the President's term had in fact upset the working balance of the Constitution, and this was apparent in the nominations to the Supreme Court. As it existed towards the close of President Franklin Roosevelt's life, it was the President's Court. All its members except one owed their appointment to the same man. It must be remembered, however, that the President's power of appointment is not unqualified; his nominations have to be confirmed by the Senate, and a hostile majority looking for ground on which to fight the President could not do better than proclaim itself the guardian of the Supreme Court's impartiality.

The claim of the Supreme Court to be the final

interpreter of the Constitution nowadays is unchallenged. Its constitutional position is that indicated by Hamilton as naturally arising out of a limited Constitution; "By a limited Constitution, I understand one which contains certain specified exceptions to the legislative authority; such, for instance, as it shall pass no Bills of Attainder, no *ex post facto laws*, and the like. Limitations of this kind can be preserved in practice no other way than through the medium of Courts of Justice, whose duty it must be to declare all acts contrary to the manifest tenor of the Constitution void. Without this, all the reservations of particular rights or privileges would amount to nothing" (*Federalist*, No. 78.). In pursuance of this doctrine State Supreme Courts already had voided acts of the State legislatures, the earliest decision of the kind going back to 1780. It was, therefore, no more than an extension of a principle already accepted that the Federal Supreme Court should declare void the acts of the Federal legislature. But in practice this must needs come to mean that the Supreme Court behaves as a sort of Second Chamber with no right of initiating legislation but with an unqualified right of veto. In England the House of Lords can prevent an Act of Parliament from coming into operation for two years;[2] in the United States an Act of Congress can go into effect and then be declared unconstitutional by the Supreme Court.

So absolute is this power of judicial veto that its exercise calls for great discretion and, in view of the

[2] See p. 73, *supra*, n.

fact that in some of its most important decisions the Court has been divided five to four, it is remarkable that there has been so little public agitation to limit its powers. The general feeling of American citizens appears to be that somebody must evidently interpret the Constitution and that an impartial interpretation is more likely to come from the Supreme Court than from any other source. The Supreme Court itself certainly has been discreet in the exercise of its powers. It will not pass judgment on an Act of Congress on its own initiative. Some person must feel himself wronged by the Act and must bring his alleged wrong to the notice of the Supreme Court before the Court will investigate the matter at all. Further, the Court has laid it down that while it is its business to determine whether Congress has the power to legislate on a particular subject, it is not concerned to enquire whether that power has been wisely exercised. The responsibility for the use of its powers rests with Congress and lies outside the Court's province.

But a further difficulty remains. The Constitution, as it itself states in its sixth Article, is a law, and the Courts, as Chief Justice Marshall laid it down, are the proper bodies to declare what the law is. In making their declaration the Courts must clearly be guided by legal principles; otherwise what they are declaring will not be law but a set of opinions, political, economic, or even individual, disguised as law. Where then are the Courts to find the legal principles that will determine their particular declarations of what the law is? It is at this point that the practice of the

Supreme Court makes contact with the British legal traditions. In "Iolanthe" the Lord Chancellor introduces himself with the observation that

> "The law is the true embodiment
> Of everything that's excellent.
> It has no kind of fault or flaw
> And I, My Lords, embody the law."

These words might have fallen from the lips of Chief Justice Coke, and though Chief Justice Marshall was less personally assertive, it is as the embodiment of, at any rate, one branch of the law—the law of the American Constitution—that he looms so large in American history.

But what in the last resort is the law? Chief Justice Coke had no doubt whatever about the answer to that question. The law was the common law and when the House of Lords sought to amend the Petition of Right by words reserving the King's sovereign authority, Coke retorted: "Magna Carta is such a fellow that he has no sovereign." But Magna Carta was common law, that is to say it claimed to be the precise statement of established custom. The rival to Common law was Roman law which had seeped into English jurisprudence via the Courts of Equity. One of the great principles of Roman Law was that the sovereign's pleasure has the force of law. It is true that Roman Law maintained that the sovereign was a law-giver because his authority derived from the people and it could thus be claimed that custom, which is popular law, inspired Roman law at one remove.

But on the face of it, custom and the King's word cannot both be supreme and when they contradict one another, one of the two must prevail. This was the problem that confronted the English judges when various taxation cases culminating in Ship-Money came before the Courts in the first forty years of the seventeenth century. No doubt some of the judges were influenced in their decisions by the fact that they owed their places to the King's pleasure, but the legal controversy that they had to determine was real enough. Custom laid it down that the redress of grievances must precede supply and that the King would therefore receive no revenues without the consent of Parliament; but the text-books laid it down that the King's prerogative was absolutely unlimited and there was evidence in English history of the full use of the prerogative, though perhaps its exercise was admitted only in times of emergency. Being lawyers the judges found it hard to go against the text-books and the King got a favourable judgement.[3]

Eventually Parliament set the verdict aside and determined by statute the principles governing the right to tax, and from that moment the judges' difficulties were really at an end. Parliament is sovereign and its pleasure has the force of law. All that the British Courts have to do when they interpret an Act of Parliament is to decide the exact legal meaning of its language. If Parliament does not like that mean-

---

[3] For the Ship-Money case consult the collection "Constitutional Documents of the Puritan Revolution" by Gardiner, pp. 105-115, 189-192.

ing, it can alter the law. When, for example, in the
Scottish Church case of some forty years ago, the
House of Lords decided that the property of the
Church belonged to a small minority, it knew that it
was giving a decision that Parliament would have to
correct, and some at least of the law lords may have
been equally conscious of the need for amending
legislation when in 1905 they decided that the Trade
Union acts of the 1870s did not mean what they had
hitherto been assumed to mean. Accordingly, when
an English court of law construes an act, it does not
admit as evidence the reports of debates or other matter indicating the intentions of Parliament; all it is
concerned to determine is what Parliament has actually said in legal language. In the United States, on
the other hand, the remedy of amending legislation
does not lie to hand. If an Act of Congress violates
the Constitution, the Constitution itself must be
changed before such an Act can become law, and the
process of constitutional change is long and difficult.
In pronouncing upon an Act of Congress, therefore,
the Supreme Court admits all the political evidence
that an English Court would exclude. It is anxious to
ascertain whether the intention of Congress was to
keep within the limits laid down by the Constitution
and once it is satisfied as to the legislature's intentions
it will do its utmost to interpret an act in accordance
with them.

Even this, however, is not enough. The Constitution dates in the main from 1787 and though a few
obscure points have been cleared up by subsequent

legislation, ingenuity and recourse to the favourite device of legal fiction are required to fit the Constitution to the vastly different circumstances of our own day. The Court must thus go behind the Constitution and enquire into the known or presumed intentions of its authors. It was certainly their intention to restrict government to a minimum. Ideas of individual freedom were in the air and, though the Constitution was careful to limit the authority of the new bodies that it created, the first Congress was not satisfied with the safeguards of individual rights that it provided, and strengthened them by the first ten amendments. The Fifth of these amendments declares that no person shall be "deprived of life, liberty or property without due process of law." The Fourteenth Amendment to the Constitution, passed after the Civil War, extended this last provision to the actions of the States. What then is due process of law? An English Court has no difficulty in answering the question because any Act of Parliament is due process. An Act of Congress, however, that violates the Constitution, is not law at all, and it will violate the Constitution if it impinges upon life, liberty or property without due process as safeguarded by the Fifth and Fourteenth Amendments.

It was once actually ruled that an act prohibiting night labour in New York bakeries was void because it trespassed upon the liberty of contract, and by an extension of the principle laid down in that decision it would have been impossible either for Congress or for any State legisature to regulate wages or hours of labour. That particular decision was got round by the convenient concept of the police power inherent in all governments. This and other instances of the same type tend to show that in decisions in regard to matters about which the Constitution is silent, and particularly about the social legislation inspired by economic circumstances of which the authors of the Constitution could have had no conception, the decisions of the Court will be shaped consciously or unconsciously by the opinions of the judges on the requirements of a social order. They will thus have to be guided by their conceptions of right reason—a term that, for all its philosophic sound, means that the judges may take generally accepted views, even if these are of comparatively recent growth, instead of the language of the common law, as their standard of reference. Recourse to ideas based on right reason was peculiarly obnoxious to Englishmen because it had so often enabled judges in the Court of Equity to substitute the principles of Roman law for the precedents of Common law and thus to cast doubt upon the traditional liberty of the subject. Clarendon expressed the average Englishmen's view when he condemned the judges of the earlier Stuart period because they "had submitted the difficulties and mysteries of the law to be measured by the standard of what they called general reason." (*History of the Rebellion* I. 64).

The situation was even richer in danger in America because American judges could not appeal to Roman law with the same confidence as had been shown by

M

their predecessors, often canonically trained, in mediaeval England. Their conceptions of right reason did
not rest upon the sure foundation of Roman law as
taken over by the Church, but were derived from
theories of society that, obeying the impulses of contemporary thought, could and did vary, not merely
from one age to another but between one party and
another. This is the truth that lay behind Justice
Oliver Wendell Holmes' acid observation to the address of his colleagues that the Constitution did not
enact Mr. Herbert Spencer's *Social Statics*. It is also
the truth that lies behind the observation of Mr. Doo-
ley, an imaginary Chicago Irishman created by a
highly-gifted journalist, Mr. W. J. Dunne, towards
the end of last century, that the Supreme Court follows the election returns. Because government is by
the consent of the governed, a Constitution must re-
spond to the ideas of those who live under it or it will
not survive. How far the American Constitution can
adjust itself to circumstances and ideas as they change,
it is for the Supreme Court to say; and how far the
Supreme Court correctly estimates and reflects contemporary opinion about the more fundamental matters of government depends upon the personality and
the political outlook of the Presidents who nominate
its members.

THE TWO EXAMPLES

T HE fundamental difference between the British and the American Constitutions lies in their respective solutions of the problem of establishing a responsible executive. It is the cardinal problem of politics. For the average man the executive is the government, and if the executive is not responsible, its acts will register the will of the master and not the consent of the governed. If, on the contrary, the executive is continuously responsible, it may lack the power to act in a crisis and this was, in fact, the besetting weakness of the Third French Republic and constitutes a danger to all federal governments in so far as their authority is indubitably limited. The English solution of the problem was accomplished by stages, not all of them visible while they were taking place, over a long period of time. On the one hand the Tudor sovereigns, and especially Henry VIII, felt a sense of responsibility to the extent of carrying Parliament with them in their policy. On the other hand Queen Victoria maintained that certain matters, particularly international affairs, still lay within the province of the Crown. Here, as in so many British constitutional arrangements, there is a penumbra that remains obscure until circumstances make its dissipation necessary. Nevertheless, the main lines of the English conception of executive responsibility are perfectly clear. It has been achieved by transferring executive power from the Crown to the Cabinet and by making the Cabinet responsible to Parliament and particularly to the House of Commons as representing the people.

This process has been gradual throughout the last three centuries and in its later stages has been smooth. But its earlier stages involved the greatest storms in English constitutional history, a civil war and a change of dynasty among them. These tumults have left their mark. The Englishman prides himself on what one of his philosophers has called "the inevitability of gradualness" and one of his poets has more picturesquely described as "freedom slowly broadening down—fromp precedent to precedent." But there is one point in the process that calls for a constitutional leap in the dark. It is the point of transition from representative to responsible Government, and it is this point that the Englishman has found it difficult to pass.

With the loss of the American colonies to give direction to its thought, British liberalism in the first half of the nineteenth century was disposed to equate full responsible Government with independence. The colonies, it was held, would drop off like ripe fruits. But as time went on and the colonies did not drop off, as, on the contrary, the significance of the Crown as a symbol of union grew steadily more apparent during

Queen Victoria's long reign, the current of thought was reversed. The colonies would not become independent but neither would they achieve full self-government. They would develop into oversea Britains associated with their parent and example by some sort of federal tie through which the ancient Parliament in London would grow into an effective agency of Imperial rule. The rise of what at the end of the last century was called colonial nationalism challenged this conception and in the years before 1914 the future organisation of the Empire had again become an open question. The course of the war answered it, and before the armistice the conception of Dominion status was well established though some years were to elapse before it was stated in legislative terms by the Statute of Westminster.

The further step that made Dominion status attainable by peoples with whom Britain stood in a more authoritative relationship than with settlers of her own or with kindred blood was taken with unexpected ease. In 1917 full self-government was stated to be the goal of British policy in India and by 1935 an Act completely transferring sovereignty to a federalised India had passed the British Parliament. The outbreak of another war found it partially in force. Responsibility for law and order in the Provinces of British India had been transferred to Ministries responsible to local legislatures, but it had not been found possible to put the plans for the Central Government into effect, and after the Japanese surrender the establishment of a unified All-Indian Government proved impracticable. So fully, however, was sovereignty conferred by the Act of 1935 that it was sufficient to make its provisions applicable to each of the two Dominions set up in 1947. The conclusion had already been drawn that Dominion status could equally be attained by the Crown Colonies. Here, however, the process was slightly more gradual. The first stage, already accomplished in Ceylon and Malta and almost accomplished in Jamaica, has been to set up a local government responsible to a House elected by universal suffrage, whose authority over all matters except defence and foreign policy is qualified only by the retention of emergency powers in the Governor's hands. Ceylon is entering on the final stage under which these reserve powers will disappear and the only question now outstanding is that of Britain's continued responsibility for the defence of a community that numbers less than 7,000,000 and is therefore unable to guarantee its own independence.

It has taken two great wars with their new distribution of material strength within the British Commonwealth, their test of the stability of the whole Imperial structure and their call for a fresh approach to old problems, to bring about developments which in retrospect seem to follow inevitably from the nature of the relationship between the Crown and the peoples under its sway. All the other steps had been easy— the initial establishment over against the executive of a Council with nominated membership and advisory functions; the introduction of an elective element; the gradual extension of the franchise; the no less gradual

transformation of the Council from an advisory body
into a genuine legislature. But throughout these
stages the executive Government has held powers in
reserve and their transfer cannot be gradual. Two
hands cannot wield one sceptre and if final authority
is to pass from the Crown's officials to the people's
representatives, it must pass at a stroke.

Under the American system this difficult transition
is evaded altogether. The American Constitution
makes the executive immediately responsible to the
people by the process of a Presidential election every
four years. Between elections the President is in a
strict sense irresponsible but he is subject to effective
restraints. He must keep within the limits of the
functions assigned to him by the Constitution, which
he has sworn to maintain, and he must look to Congress for all legislation, including supply. The constitutional position of an American President was
perfectly comprehended by Lincoln. By proclamation he had suspended the Habeas Corpus Act and
by proclamation he had freed the slaves. If, by proclamation, Lincoln had postponed the Presidential election on the ground of the war emergency, it is hard
to see who could have said him nay. In spite of the
Constitution there is a penumbra about the Presidential
power. The Constitution declares the President Commander-in-Chief of the American Army and Navy.
The powers of a Commander-in-Chief are of necessity
indefinable; he must take such action as emergencies
demand. Lincoln's powers as Commander-in-Chief
were in full operation as he approached the end of his

first term and he regarded it as his duty under the Constitution to maintain the Union at all costs. He was to be opposed at the forthcoming election by one of his own unsuccessful generals, and there was, at the very least, a likelihood that his opponent would be elected. So gloomy, in fact, was the prospect that the State of Nevada was hurriedly created in order to assure Lincoln an additional three votes in the electoral college. Lincoln knew that if he failed to secure re-election, his opponent would open peace negotiations with the South and that the cause for which he fought would be lost. Nevertheless, he held that under the Constitution his authority was limited in time, that unless he were re-elected in November 1864 he would become a mere private person on March 4, 1865, and that if the presidential election were postponed by his order the country would, in law, be without an executive government at all after that date. Accordingly, Lincoln felt it absolutely necessary that the election should go forward in the usual way. He even formed plans, with which he acquainted his Cabinet, for his conduct in the event of his defeat to ease the transition of power during the four months between the election and the expiry of his term. The preservation of the Union was a great thing but the preservation of American democracy was a greater.

The difficulty of harmonising continuity of policy with freedom of electoral choice with which Lincoln was thus confronted—which also caused Wilson so much embarrassment during and after the Paris Peace Conference of 1919, and which may have helped to induce President Roosevelt to break the third term convention—arises out of the feature of the American system that identifies the head of the State with the head of a party in the State.[1] This is the penalty that America pays not so much perhaps for the election of a President by the people as for the failure of the Founding Fathers to allow for the play of party feelings and to devise election machinery that would take them into account. In England the Crown is beyond party and a change of party government can therefore be accomplished with less of a jolt under English than under American institutions. But under either system the effects of the changes, if followed out to their logical conclusion and if there were any fundamental difference between the parties, would result in anarchy. Fortunately the common sense of both peoples saves them from logic.

Lincoln's argument, which has been endorsed by posterity, assumes that the President is the choice of the American people. So in practice he is, though with certain qualifications, but such was not the intention of the members of the Philadelphia Convention. The French Revolution had begun to cast its shadow when the Convention met, and democracy

---

[1] The perplexity in which this arrangement involves ordinary Americans is illustrated by the story of the American soldier who asked his sergeant what he could do to make an obstinately hidden Japanese sniper come out into the open. "Try shouting something offensive at him" advised the sergeant. The soldier went off but returned presently to report failure. "I shouted out 'To hell with Hirohito' and he jumped out at once and shouted back 'To hell with Roosevelt,' and I couldn't shoot another Republican, could I?"

was in the air. The fathers of the Constitution, all of them good solid propertied men, thoroughly distrusted it. To them, as to Queen Victoria in her letters, "democratic" was synonymous with "revolutionary" and there is a striking passage in one of Madison's papers (*Federalist*, No. 10) in which he urges that the more comprehensive the Union, the less are democratic excesses likely to infect it. With a direct reference to agitations hardly stilled, he wrote that "a rage for paper money, for an abolition of debts, for an equal division of property, or for any other improper or wicked project, will be less apt to pervade the whole body of the union than any particular member of it," and the argument was bound to appeal to the voters, all of them at the time men of property, to whose approval the Constitution was referred.

Elaborate arrangements were devised to shelter a Presidential election from the gusts of popular feeling. It was intended that the President should be chosen by the House of Representatives from a list of candidates drawn up by the States. Each State was to elect a body of electors equal in number to its representation in both Houses and therefore never less than three. These electors were to meet in their respective States and decide on the names of two candidates; and in order to prevent the electors from confronting Congress with twenty-six different names, each of them borne by a distinguished person in the State concerned, it was provided that of the two candidates chosen "one at least shall not be an inhabitant of the same State with themselves." If when the votes were brought together, one candidate had an absolute majority he would become President. Otherwise, the House would choose the President out of the five highest names on the list. In 1800 the election resulted in a tie and the House then chose Jefferson to be President. This election led to a constitutional amendment, the Twelfth, under which the electors voted separately for the President and the Vice-President and the number of candidates submitted to the House was reduced to three. It was under this arrangement that in 1824 the House made Adams President in succession to Monroe. His votes were well behind those of the candidate at the head of the list but the House chose him as the result of a deal by his supporters with the supporters of a candidate for the Vice-Presidency.

This episode led to the assertion that the voice of the people was being ignored and to the development of parties that would choose at their conventions candidates whose names would be binding upon all the electors whose return they secured. The arrangement still holds good and the candidate who secures a majority of the members of the electoral college, all of them already pledge-bound, is in fact elected, the rest of the proceedings being purely formal. Even before 1824 the procedure contemplated by the authors of the Constitution had not operated. Members of Congress had met in Presidential caucuses and had chosen their respective candidates, their choice being respected by the electors in the States, who voted as they were told by Congress, and when the behaviour of Congress became obnoxious to public opinion, voted as they were told by the party managers.

Under the present system, which makes the electors men of straw, survivals of a past that had in fact never been a present, it could be claimed that the President is in truth the people's choice, were it not that the election is by States. In the electoral college a State cannot record a split vote. Its delegation votes as a whole for one candidate or the other. Thus a few votes in a State may determine the complexion of its whole delegation. In 1916 Wilson was re-elected because he carried California by a narrow margin. The effect of this arrangement is that the minority vote in those States whose party allegiance is constant has no effect whatever on the result. In 1936 Mr. Roosevelt's opponent carried only two States, the faithful remnant of the once solidly Republican North-East, and he therefore commanded a mere handful of votes in the electoral college. Nevertheless 15 million people supported him at the polls. It is thus possible for an American President to be elected by a minority of the voters because the more thinly-populated States are over-represented in the electoral college.[2] The strength of their delegation is that of their representation in both Houses of Congress, and every State whatever its size has two Senators. The abolition of the electoral college and the substitution of election by

---

[2] This actually happened in two cases, namely Hayes in 1876 and Harrison in 1888. Hayes' popular vote was 300,000 smaller than that of his opponent Tilden and Harrison's 100,000 smaller than Cleveland's.

direct popular vote would give a great stimulus to the activities of both parties in the regions in which they are weakest. It may become a possibility of the future now that the development of social service is restricting the field of patronage in which the parties have hitherto operated with so much effect.

The election of a President, whether the method be indirect as was originally intended or direct as it has now largely become, makes it impossible for the executive power to be vested in the Cabinet. Under the American Constitution all executive power belongs to the President and the members of his Cabinet are his departmental subordinates. The text-books quote the story of Lincoln taking a vote in his Cabinet on a measure that he had proposed. All the Cabinet were against it. "Seven Noes," said Lincoln, and then, putting up his own hand, "one Aye. The Ayes have it." That was sound constitutional arithmetic. A man of whom it can be said, though in a qualified sense, that he has been chosen by the people to hold power cannot transfer his responsibilities to his associates. The English system of Cabinet government is constitutionally impossible in the United States, and because of this impossibility the executive cannot be made responsible to the legislature. Instead he is directly responsible to the people. The English system has the advantage in facilitating day-to-day control, the American is bringing home to the average voter the conviction that he determines his country's policies.

It is among the curiosities of constitutional study

that the vast difference both in the practical working of the two systems and in the popular attitude towards them should not emerge from an examination of the relevant documents. On paper, executive power in both countries is centred in an individual—in Britain in the King, in America in the President. But the machinery of election that on one side of the Atlantic survives only in certain traditional forms is on the other—not because of the Constitution but in spite of it—the greatest of political realities. It is therefore impossible for a President to divest himself of his powers. He can, and indeed in practice must, assign their detailed exercise to subordinates and his discretion in distributing them is limited by legislation establishing a number of departments. But the President can assign specific duties to individuals without obtaining congressional authority and in war-time makes ample use of this power. The sole condition for its exercise is that his nominee remains individually responsible to him and to him alone. It follows that no power whatever is vested in the Cabinet as such and its omission from the machinery of government set up by the Constitution is logical enough. Indeed, if the first President had treated the Senate as his Council, which is probably what the authors of the Constitution intended, no Cabinet would have come into existence. But Cabinet Government was already a part of the English tradition in 1776; day-to-day co-operation between President and Senate would at once have raised the delicate question of the balance of authority between the Federal Government and the States; and in operating a new constitution it was clearly desirable for the relationship between the President and his closest advisers to be given definite form. The appointment of a Cabinet just met the need, and the precedent set has been followed. But since an American Cabinet is made up of persons individually responsible to the President,[3] it is incapable of development as an institution. It remains what it was 150 years ago—a group of persons whom the President consults collectively at his pleasure. But apart from him it has no authority even to meet and when, during Wilson's illness, his Secretary of State called a meeting on his own initiative, the President at once dismissed him.

In Britain, on the other hand, the Cabinet is the keystone of the constitutional arch, the essential link between Crown and Parliament, which alone renders the King incapable of doing wrong and the House of Commons capable of determining policy. It was with the shaping of policy that the Cabinet was originally concerned. Partly for this reason and partly because of the significance of party in the evolution of English politics, its responsibility is collective. The Prime Minister determines its membership, but once they are appointed they are his colleagues not his subordinates, and it is to the House of Commons rather than to him that they are responsible for the conduct of their respective departments. The British

---

[3] The Confederate Constitution empowered its Congress to legislate for the presence of Cabinet Ministers on the floor of either House; but advantage was not taken of this provision.

Cabinet is an admirable instrument of decision on major issues and is thus strong where the American Cabinet is powerless, but it has experienced great difficulty in establishing a hold on administration. In Victorian times the Cabinet consisted of a number of gentlemen of similar political views meeting once a week for private and unrecorded discussions of matters of common interest. The South African war revealed, as the Crimean war had done before it, the hiatus that thus existed between ministerial decision and departmental action; and to remedy this defect in the field in which it was most dangerous, Mr. Balfour, when Prime Minister, established the Committee of Imperial Defence. This body, of which the Prime Minister was the one permanent member, was the means of providing the Cabinet with the material required for correlating means with ends. In the First World War it was expanded into the War Committee of the Cabinet. In the Second World War it was reduced to the Chiefs of Staff Committee, reporting to the Prime Minister as Minister of Defence. Its functions and indeed its existence in the world of tomorrow will depend on the situation with which the Cabinets of to-morrow will be called upon to deal. In this important field the evolution of the Cabinet is still incomplete.

The Cabinet's position in domestic politics is equally transitional. Its size has always depended on circumstances, and in the half century before 1914 gradually increased from an average of 10 to an average of 20. In 1916 Mr. Lloyd George formed a War

Cabinet of 4 members, all free of departmental duties.
The Chancellor of the Exchequer, though a member,
was not expected to attend regularly. Other Ministers were summoned when matters affecting their
departments were under discussion, but only the Foreign Secretary was constantly present. It was clearly
necessary to create a proper channel for the convey-
ance of Cabinet decisions to the administrative departments, and to this end Mr. Lloyd George set up
the Cabinet Secretariat. This body has now become
one of the most important organs in the State. It regu-
lates the distribution of business, sees to it that nothing comes up to the Cabinet that can be settled at the
departmental level, and is replacing the Treasury as
the authority supervising and co-ordinating the conduct of public affairs. Its future, too, is uncertain.
War, with its need for quick decisions, calls for small
Cabinets. In peacetime it has hitherto been found
more convenient to appoint large Cabinets, which,
because of their size, can set up Committees to handle
detailed issues. Both forms are compatible with the
principles of Cabinet Government and the eventual
choice between small and large Cabinets may well
depend on a future Prime Minister's temperament.

In the actual working of both Constitutions, convention—in the English sense of the word—plays a considerable part. It is, for example, a matter of common
convention that a Bill is *read three times*—a conven-

N

tion taken over into the United States Congress from
Colonial precedents, reinforced by Jefferson's "Man-
ual of Parliamentary Practice," which drew heavily
on English sources. But convention is even more important under the English system. Convention has
deprived the Crown of its powers to veto acts of the
British parliament, and its veto over the acts of Dominion parliaments had in fact lapsed by convention
before it was formally set aside by the Statute of Westminster in 1931. In the United States, where constitutional powers are more closely defined by statute, the
field is smaller, but there were throughout the nineteenth century two conventions that profoundly affected the development of the Constitution. The first,
which derives from Washington, was that a President
could not hold office for more than two terms. The
Constitution is silent on the question of re-eligibility,
though it was much discussed in the Philadelphia
sessions, and by its silence implicitly permits it. Hamilton, in one of his most powerful papers (*Federalist*,
No. 72) assumes that a President will offer himself
for re-election and details the consequent advantages
to the nation. Washington refused to offer himself
for re-election more than once, and the precedent
that he set was followed for nearly 150 years. The
second convention dates from Washington's successor,
Jefferson, who held that a President's messages to
Congress should be communicated in writing and not
in person. Washington had somewhat over-awed Congress, and Jefferson felt that the President's personal
appearance to urge legislation upon that body was

an infraction of the principle of the separation of powers. This convention also obtained for more than a century.

It is significant of the real fluidity of political life in the United States within the apparently rigid framework of the Constitution that both conventions have now lapsed. The second was broken by President Wilson, who resumed the practice of delivering Presidential messages in person within a few years of his statement in his book *The State* that the convention of the written message was well established. The two-term convention was of greater importance and was harder to overthrow. Perhaps, indeed, it might never have been overthrown from within. It is true that there was talk of a third term for Grant, but when the President understood that Congress was hostile, he dropped the idea. There was also talk of a third term for Cleveland, and in 1897 his opponents met the suggestion with a strong resolution: "We declare it to be the unwritten law of this Republic established by custom and usage of 100 years and sanctioned by the example of the greatest and wisest of those who founded and have maintained our government, that no man shall be eligible for a third term of the Presidential office." But Lincoln had uttered a famous warning against swapping horses whilst crossing a stream, and President Roosevelt acted upon it when he offered himself for a third term in the course of a war which even then threatened to engulf the United States. It is to be noted that his language in submitting himself for a fourth term was rather that of a Commander-in-Chief than that of a President; but if war creates precedents, peace tends to confirm them.[4]

———————◆◆◆◆———————

No constitutional arrangements, whether written or unwritten, can provide for all contingencies, and there must somewhere be a reserve power capable of dealing with crises when they occur. The Third French Republic had in the course of time seen such a concentration of power in the hands of the Chamber of Deputies that there was no reserve left, with the result that the Constitution collapsed with the army. In England, reserve power still resides in the Crown: "The King's government must be carried on," and in the last resort the King himself must see that it is carried on. Queen Victoria's action to prevent a constitutional break-down through a conflict between the two Houses of Parliament over Irish disestablishment has become classical, and the troubled reign of King George V provided four instances of direct political action by the Sovereign. The first occurred in 1910 when the House of Lords rejected the Parliament Bill and a deadlock was reached, which could be overcome only by the Crown's willingness to make a large creation of peers. Here the circumstances of 1832 provided a useful precedent. It is the business of the Crown to give effect to the will of the people and when its intervention is called for the Crown is entitled to ask that the will of the people shall be ex-

———————

[4] See, however, p. 77 *supra*, n., regarding the latest development.

pressed in unmistakable fashion. A General Election
fought on the specific issue that it will require action
by the Crown to settle, gives the Sovereign just that
indication of the popular will that he desires, and an
election was fought on the Parliament Bill in 1910,
just as it was fought on the Reform Bill in 1832. The
action of the Crown in requiring a second election in
1910, although the Liberal government had been confirmed in office by the first election of that year, was
criticised at the time from the Left, just as its action
as a consequence of the election in giving Ministers its
undertaking to create peers was criticised from the
Right; but long before the end of the King's reign
there was general agreement that the Crown's behaviour had been thoroughly constitutional.

The next instance of the Crown's intervention
occurred in 1914, when the passage of the third Home
Rule Bill threatened to cause civil war in Ireland.
The King then promoted a conference of responsible
leaders, over which he requested Mr. Speaker to preside, in order to explore the possibilities of an eleventh
hour settlement. The conference proved abortive and
the Irish dispute moved forward to an issue that few
had dreamt of in 1914. Thirdly, in the autumn of
1916, the break-up of the Coalition Government under
Mr. Asquith created an abnormal situation. Under
normal conditions there is a constitutional opposition
ready to take office when called upon and the Crown
is in no doubt as to the quarter in which to look for
a Prime Minister; but the Coalition effected in 1915
had absorbed the opposition into the government and

the Crown had itself to determine who was best qualified to carry on the war to a victorious end in accordance with the undoubted will of the people. The
King's choice of Mr. Lloyd George determined the
composition of the new Ministry. Finally, in 1931,
when the economic depression overwhelmed the country and when events could not wait for a government
comprehensive enough to cope with it to be formed
by the slow process of a general election, the King's
intervention caused the Conservative and Liberal
leaders to accept office in an administration formed
by the Labour Prime Minister.

This matter of a residue of emergency powers by
whatever agency they are exercised causes peculiar
difficulty in federal constitutions because by its very
nature a federal constitution limits the power of the
central government. In Canada the difficulty is overcome by a clause in the British North America Act
giving the Dominion Government general authority
to legislate for the peace, order and good government of the country. In Australia, where the powers
of the Commonwealth government are severely cir-
cumscribed, provision was made for their extension
by the agreement of the State legislatures or, alternatively, by referendum. In the United States the
authors of the Constitution sought to meet possible
future needs by setting up the machinery for constitutional amendment. But the Constitution itself was an
emergency device; it set out to give the country an
effective central government such as was not provided
for in the Articles of Confederation. The Articles

established no executive. The Constitution repaired
the omission and under the Constitution the executive
is the President. There has thus been latent in the
Presidency from the very first a certain reserve of
power that Jefferson drew upon when he carried
through the Louisiana Purchase and that Lincoln
drew upon when he issued his Emancipation Proclamation. To some extent, therefore, the Presidency is
an emergency symbol. In the period of quiet progress
that succeeded the civil war the President's importance
was subordinate to that of Congress, and Bryce, writing at the height of this period, though after the Constitution had been in operation for a full century, even
thought it worth while to note the suggestion that the
Presidency could be abolished on the ground that its
work was done.

No one would advance such a suggestion now. It is
the Vice-President whose position is now called in
question. He has certain constitutional resemblance
to an English Prince of Wales; so long as he holds his
position he has nothing definite to do, unless the President dies, when he becomes the head of the State.
It is true that he is the official Chairman of the Senate
but, as he is not a member of that body, he leaves all
important rulings to be settled by the Senators and if
he is not interested in debates, he is content to allow a
Senator to replace him in the Chair. At the time the
Constitution was drawn up the Senate was thought of
rather as a Council working in close co-operation
with the President, and it is possible that the Vice-
President was intended to serve as a direct link

between the executive and the senior branch of the legislature. When, however, during Jefferson's Vice-
Presidency, it was suggested to him that he might
enter the President's Cabinet, he repudiated the idea
as incompatible with the separation of powers. And
as Vice-Presidents are usually men of no particular
distinction, no subsequent attempt has been made to
give constitutional significance to their office. It is
possible, however, that here, too, the break with the
two-term convention may accelerate a change of
which there are already indications. On taking office
in 1921 President Harding invited the Vice-President
to attend meetings of his Cabinet, thus establishing a
new precedent, which President Truman has further
extended. The latter's accession to the presidential
office having left the Vice-Presidency vacant, he has
invited the President pro tempore of the Senate to
attend Cabinet meetings. In 1945 as in 1921 the object
of the innovation was to induce agreement between
President and Senate in regard to treaties.

This doctrine, or rather dogma, of the separation of
powers constituted the sheet anchor of American
thought throughout the turbulent period in which independence was achieved and the Constitution
brought into being. In times of great uncertainty,
men's minds require a formula the constant assertion
of which will give them their required sense of direction. "Redress of grievances must precede supply"
served England well throughout her formative period; "separation of powers" served the United States
equally well during the last quarter of the 18th cen-

tury. In 1780 Massachusetts declared in its Constitution that the separation of powers guaranteed the rule of law instead of the rule of men, and in 1800, in his farewell address, Washington warned his hearers that "the spirit of encroachment tends to consolidate the powers of all departments in one and thus to create, whatever the form of government, a real despotism."

This formula for the assurance of individual freedom stemmed from Montesquieu whose *Esprit des Lois*, published in 1748, was the first thorough-going attempt to derive a philosophy of history from the historical record and rightly took immediate rank as a classic. Montesquieu had visited England in 1730, arriving shortly after Voltaire had left, and brought away with him after his 18 months' stay a lasting admiration for the British Constitution as the sole example in the world of his day of the successful reconciliation of order with liberty. This reconciliation, he argued, was based on the total separation and mutual independence of the three main departments of government, the Executive, the Legislature and the Judiciary.

The controversies of Stuart times had in truth brought home to the English people the necessity of an independent judicature. It was indispensable to the effective redress of grievances; for if a subject of the Crown felt himself wronged, he looked to the Courts —Parliament itself was in its origins mainly a Court—for his remedy, and if the Courts were rendered powerless to give it to him, he lacked all safeguards against oppression. The independence of the judiciary was finally secured by the Revolution settlement, which set aside the doctrine that judges held their appointment during pleasure. So far, then, Montesquieu interpreted English constitutional practice rightly, though, in fact, the separation of judicature and executive is not and has never been complete. The Lord Chancellor, who is head of the judiciary, is a member of the government, and it is a convention that the Attorney General has a claim to the office of Lord Chief Justice if it falls vacant during his term of office. Nevertheless, the English are right in their view that on the whole the Courts have nothing to do with politics. Lord Chancellors and Attorneys General are lawyers who have become politicians, and when they return to their professions they readily become lawyers again. Where Montesquieu erred was in supposing that the principle of the separation of powers also governed the relations of executive and legislature. In fact the two are organically linked by the doctrine of Cabinet responsibility, and when Montesquieu was in England, Walpole had already come to power and the final structure of the Constitution was beginning to reveal itself.

But though Montesquieu failed to note the constitutional tendency already in process of development, his error was not so great in 1730 as it must needs appear now. After the Revolution the chief fear of the House of Commons was that its newly asserted position should be undermined by the appearance on its benches of men who owed their appointments to the

Crown and who therefore looked to it for instructions. A bill excluding place-men, as they were called, was passed in 1693 and vetoed by the King; passed again in 1694, and rejected by the House of Lords; finally passed in 1705, and repealed three years later. Nevertheless 1705 is one of the most important dates in English constitutional history, for the repeal of the Act passed in that year was accomplished by a characteristic English compromise. It was provided that offices of profit under the Crown created subsequently to 1705 should be incompatible with membership of the House of Commons and that the holders of offices created before that year should vacate their seats but should be eligible for re-election. It was intended by these means to prevent the Crown from debauching the House of Commons through the multiplication of place-men. The date-line drawn was arbitrary; the real test clearly ought to be the character of the office and not the time of its creation; and in 1741 another Act excluded from the House of Commons the holders of a number of offices which had existed prior to 1705. By the time of George III's accession, however, the eligibility of most office-holders for re-election had transferred the threat to the independence of the House of Commons from the appointments themselves to the constituencies for which their holders sat. In 1782 Rockingham disfranchised the revenue officers who numbered 11,500, and by so doing is said to have deprived the Crown of the control of seventy parliamentary seats. In the nineteenth and twentieth centuries successive extensions of the franchise gradually made it impossible for constituencies to be subject to royal, aristocratic or capitalistic influences, though there are still a considerable number of seats in which the composition of the electorate, overwhelmingly well-to-do or overwhelmingly trade-unionist, makes nomination equivalent to election.

The arrangement made in 1705 is now obsolete but in its time it was of the highest constitutional importance. Had it not been made, the British civil service with its great tradition of political impartiality could hardly have come into existence; and it is not surprising that the artificial distinction between offices that existed before 1705 and those created after that date was maintained into the twentieth century. At its inception the offices, acceptance of which vacated a seat in the House of Commons, included most positions of Cabinet rank, so that an appointment to a ministerial post was followed by a by-election. Shortly before the war of 1914 Mr. Asquith's administration abolished the necessity for re-election during the first nine months of a parliament's life, thus avoiding the need for a considerable number of contests when a new government was formed just after the General Election. And in 1919 the old rule finally disappeared from the Statute Book so that now all Ministers of the Crown are members of one or other House of Parliament and need not submit themselves to re-election after accepting ministerial office.[5]

---

[5] This rule is not seriously weakened by the case of Sir Hardman Lever, who was joint Financial Secretary to the Treasury with

In the American colonies the question of the independence of the judiciary never became acute because it had been settled in England before their
political life had developed very far. The crux in
America arose out of the relations of the executive
with the legislature. Again and again royal governors,
strong in the support of the administration at home,
had over-ruled or ignored the will of the Colonial
Houses of Assembly, so that even before the Declaration of Independence it had become apparent to the
colonists that for them a free government meant the
guarantee of inalienable rights to the local legislatures.
When independence had been achieved, the States
became sovereign Commonwealths, the Continental
Congress, which was nominally the government of
the United States, being in fact composed of delegates
from the States, to which it could no more than address requests, which it had no power to enforce. The
Constitution of 1787 proposed to elect a real central
government with powers of taxation, and its opponents contended that under the provisions the old
tyranny would simply be transferred from one side

Mr. Stanley (afterwards Earl) Baldwin during the latter part of
the 1914-18 war but was never a member of Parliament. Mr.
Lloyd George considered that a political figure of some consequence was required in Washington to transact day-to-day business with the United States Treasury on behalf of the British
Treasury. He appointed an extra Financial Secretary of the
Treasury for that specific purpose. The powers of the House of
Commons, however, were not impugned; for Mr. Baldwin and his
chief, the Chancellor of the Exchequer, were members and were
answerable to the House for all actions of their department including those initiated by their colleague in Washington, Sir
Hardman Lever.

of the Atlantic to the other. The same difficulty had of course arisen in the States themselves when they had to provide governors of their own in place of governors appointed by the Crown, and it had been solved by giving the State legislatures that assured position which the colonial Assemblies had lacked. Montesquieu's doctrine of the separation of powers provided just the formula required for the solution of the problem. Everybody referred to him—it must be remembered that in the later eighteenth century the new ideas that were beginning to occupy men's minds were all of French origin—and Madison, who in one place (*Federalist*, No. 47) describes him as "the oracle who is always consulted and cited on this subject" was thoroughly familiar with his book (see in particular his paper *Federalist*, No. 43, and for Hamilton's views of him *Federalist*, No. 9). Actually, however, as Madison was perfectly well aware, Montesquieu's doctrine was not strictly applied. The President was given a qualified veto over legislation, and the Senate was associated with the President both in the conclusion of treaties and in appointments to the higher federal offices. In practice, too, the Supreme Court has not been able to interpret the Constitution without expressing itself on political issues. The English political genius has never more clearly expressed itself on both sides of the Atlantic than in its readiness to modify all general principles in detail in the very process of asserting them.

The general acceptance of the separation of powers as a guiding constitutional principle requires to be borne in mind in any estimate of the originality of the work done by the members of the Philadelphia convention. How far they themselves thought that they had a free hand is disputable. Invitations to the convention were issued by a convention that had assembled in Annapolis in the previous year. It was summoned to deal with questions of inter-State trade and was attended by delegates from only five States. Feeling that both its terms of reference and its numbers were inadequate, the Annapolis convention issued invitations to another convention at Philadelphia that was to amend the Articles of Confederation so as to make them "adequate to the exigencies of government and the preservation of the Union." This form of words gave the new convention ample powers, but the invitation was submitted to the Continental Congress, which, in agreeing to its issue, restricted the scope of the new body to a revision of the Articles of Confederation. Actually the Philadelphia convention did not concern itself with the scope of its terms of reference. It concerned itself with the facts of the situation. The experience of the last four years had made it clear that certain general controls over the thirteen States, which had been exercised by the government in London and which had lapsed with the recognition of American Independence, needed to be restored.

The situation was, in fact, the exact opposite of that which now confronts the statesmen of the British Commonwealth. For them the problem is one of ensuring complete mutual understanding without encroaching upon the real independence of their respective communities. Geography has a strong influence on history. It is impossible for a group of states scattered over the habitable globe to be governed from one centre. Even the arrangement that centred the control of foreign policy in London is breaking down with the development by the Dominions of their own foreign relationships, much as arrangements for the centralisation of Imperial defence faded out with the establishment and growth of Dominion forces. Matters of such delicacy as those that have to be dealt with by the Commonwealth Governments in their day-to-day contacts cannot be regulated by a formula or fitted into a centralised constitutional framework. They are best dealt with as they arise, in the characteristic British way. Given the will to co-operate, a will based on the conviction of ultimate unity of purpose, the means to co-operate can always be devised. In the United States, however, geography enforced centralisation. The States were continuous; therefore their respective sovereignties inevitably clashed with one another and the surrender of powers to a central regulating authority was the only alternative to political and economic chaos. With thirteen sovereign States actually in existence, the one practical method of establishing this authority was through some form of federation, and the Philadelphia convention owes its significance for the world's history to its success in expressing the idea of federation in terms suited to modern conditions.

Here it had no precedents, English or other, to

guide it; the only parallels that it could find were certain federal developments, notably the Achaean League, in the Greek world before the establishment of Roman rule, and of this material, such as it was, it made ample use. But in the main it broke new ground and, after prolonged and difficult discussions, it fought its way to the principle that a federation requires two Houses, with equal representation for all federating States in the one and unequal representation on a population basis in the other. This plan, which solved a most difficult situation by a reasonable compromise, has been taken as a model by subsequent federations, either directly, as in Australia, or indirectly, as in Canada, where the problem took a slightly different form and where Quebec, as the principal champion of States rights, secured its position by the guarantee of a certain minimum representation in the lower House. In this matter of federal organisation, then, the Philadelphia convention presented the world with a political device that was entirely new and capable of the widest application.

One of the possibilities of the early future is that it may be applied in Europe on a considerable scale. Even before the outbreak of the Second World War there were certain tendencies apparent in some European states that suggested their reorganisation on a federal instead of on a unitary basis. Observers of Spanish affairs in particular could see no other solution to that perpetual conflict between the central government and the provinces that had involved the country in a constant series of civil wars. In Italy,

O

too, it seemed that reaction against Fascism might
eventually take the form of an assertion of provincial
rights against the excessive centralisation of the country's affairs in Rome. In Russia, which, since the late
autumn of 1917 has been in name a Union of Socialist
Soviet Republics, the threat of war enforced unitary
government; but the latest constitutional reform has
given the 16 constituent Republics a freedom of action even in international affairs that makes the Soviet
Union unique among federations. In France, observers
had not failed to note how under the stress of revolutionary developments the country's earlier provincial
structure was beginning to show up in plans of political and administrative reorganisation. In Germany,
after the collapse of the Empire in 1918, the difficulties
that the preponderance of Prussia put in the way of
the functioning of a federal state were appreciated.
A more unitary form of government was adopted with
consequences that the Nazis were to make explicit.
As Nazism systematically destroyed all forms of association—political, economic, social and even to some
extent religious—which were not under its control
and animated by its spirit, the problem of the future
political structure of Germany was finally thrown
into the lap of the occupying powers. Now there is
the presumption that the disasters that centralised
control brought upon the German people have produced a reaction towards that diversity through local
autonomy that was for many centuries characteristic
of German life. At the other end of Europe, the
federal solution of the Macedonian question, long

made impossible by the mutual intolerance of local nationalists' ambitions, has been made practical politics by Marshal Tito. Finally, the idea of federalisation on the inter-European level—that is to say, the unity of Europe in a federal framework—is exercising a new fascination upon people in all countries of that di-shevelled continent. In such thoughts many take heart from the interesting example of Switzerland, where federal institutions have in a singular way given scope to the political needs of an ethnically and culturally diversified population.

Be this as it may, it is certain that the constitution-makers will look for inspiration to Britain and the United States of America, the two countries whose institutions have triumphantly survived all the tests of war. In the somewhat similar situation that arose after 1815 they all looked to England, and it was unfortunate that the doctrinaire Liberalism then in fashion held that constitution-making had become a science and that, if application were made to such a competent philosopher as Jeremy Bentham, constitutions could be handed out while you wait. To-day, or rather to-morrow, eyes will be directed to Washington and to Moscow as well as to London. More than seventy years ago, when the French National Assembly set itself to provide France with a new Constitution, its members were doubtful whether they should look across the Channel or across the Atlantic. Actually they looked in both directions. They took from England the idea of a constitutional President with its corollary of a Cabinet responsible to the legislature;

they took from America the conception of fixed terms of office as a safeguard against despotism. The Constitution of the Third Republic did indeed provide for an emergency dissolution of the Chamber, but the arrangements that it set up broke down after their first trial and it became a principle of the Constitution that the Chamber should live out its four years of life. With its existence assured, the Chamber could make and unmake cabinets at its pleasure; and the executive power was thus weakened to an extent that eventually became fatal. The temptation to draw extreme conclusions from such distressing experience has been and still is great. Yet, in the Constitution of the Fourth Republic, the French seem to have remembered well that the establishment of a strong executive may easily become the first stage on the road to autocratic rule.

The Englishman with his long tradition of opposition to personal government will assuredly continue to cherish his tradition of the day-to-day control of the executive made possible by the responsibility of the Cabinet to Parliament. The American for his part will be no less tenacious of his tradition of separate powers expressed by an independent executive held in check by quadrennial elections, under which his country has risen to her present great position in the world. There is, probably, no compromise between an executive ultimately responsible to the people and an executive continuously responsible to the people's representatives. In any case only confusion will result from comfortable platitudes about the common root of British and American institutions. Circumstances have caused them to evolve entirely different principles of growth. Parliamentary and Presidential sovereignties are not compatible with one another; and, as the powers of the federal executive are still expanding in the United States while the Commonwealth is moving towards an ever-wider distribution of authority, the chances are that the divergences between the two systems will grow wider rather than narrower as time goes on.

Acrimonious disputes prejudicial to the future tranquility of the world will be avoided if a firm hold be kept on the truth apparent to students of either the British or the American Constitution, and still more of the relationship between the two, that both have, as it were, grown out of their native soil. Local circumstances have shaped them, and local circumstances have decided whether their shape should be given them gradually or instantly. Usage has modified and even determined their working and, above all, the political sense of the peoples who live under them has continually moulded the action of those who have held their highest offices. These indigenous factors cannot be transplanted, but in their own congenial air they will continue to assert themselves and will make it as certain as anything can be in this changeable world that both Constitutions will continue to develop on their own lines and in accordance with their own inner spirit, always reaching towards the same ends by diverse means but always holding out to free men the hope and promise of free lives in a free world.

SELECTED
BIBLIOGRAPHY

Cases in Constitutional Law, D. L. Keir and F. H. Lawson. Clarendon Press, Oxford and Oxford University Press, New York, 1928.

Select Documents of English Constitutional History, G. B. Adams and H. M. Stephens. The Macmillan Co., London and New York, 1924.

ENGLISH

Magna Carta, by W. S. McKechnie. James Maclehose & Sons, Glasgow, 1905, second edition, 1914.

Select Charters and other Illustrations of English Constitutional History from the Earliest Times to the Reign of Edward I, by William Stubbs, Bishop of Oxford, sometime Regius Professor of Modern History in the University of Oxford. Clarendon Press, Oxford.

Select Statutes and other Constitutional Documents Illustrative of the Reigns of Elizabeth and James I, by G. W. Prothero, Professor of History in the University of Edinburgh and Hon. Fellow of King's College, Cambridge. Clarendon Press, Oxford, 1898.

The Constitutional Documents of the Puritan Revolution, 1625-1660, by S. R. Gardiner, Fellow of Merton College, Oxford. Clarendon Press, 1899.

Select Statutes, Cases and Documents to Illustrate English Constitutional History, 1660-1832, by Sir Charles Grant Robertson, Fellow of All Souls College, Ox-

ford. Methuen, London, 1904. (The second edition
of this, published in 1913, contains the text of the
Parliament Act of 1911 and a number of very important cases decided in the Courts subsequent to 1832.)

AMERICAN

Documents of American History, second edition,
H. S. Commager (Editor). F. S. Crofts & Company,
New York, 1940.

Records of the Federal Convention, four volumes,
Max Farrand (Editor). Yale University Press, New
Haven, 1937.

The Federalist, edition by Paul L. Ford. Henry Holt
and Company, New York, 1898.

Leading Constitutional Decisions, seventh edition,
Robert E. Cushman. F. S. Crofts & Company, New
York, 1944.

The Growth of American Constitutional Law, Benjamin F. Wright. Henry Holt and Company, New
York, 1942.

Introduction to American Government, ninth edition,
F. A. Ogg and P. O. Ray. D. Appleton-Century Company, Inc., New York, 1948.

*Principles and Functions of Government in the United
States*, W. Leon Godshall (Editor). D. Van Nostrand
Company, Inc., New York, 1948.

The People, Politics, and the Politician, A. N. Chris-
tensen and E. M. Kirkpatrick (Editors). Henry Holt
and Company, New York, 1941.

Source Book on the Government of England, R. K.
Gooch. D. Van Nostrand Company, Inc., New York,
1930.

INDEX